Hiking New Mexico's Chaco Canyon
The Trails, the Ruins, the History

Hiking New Mexico's Chaco Canyon
The Trails, the Ruins, the History

James C. Wilson

SUNSTONE
PRESS

SANTA FE

Sunstone books may be purchased for educational, business, or sales promotional use.
For information please write: Special Markets Department, Sunstone Press,
P.O. Box 2321, Santa Fe, New Mexico 87504-2321.

Book and cover design › R. Ahl

Library of Congress Cataloging-in-Publication Data

Names: Wilson, James C. (James Calmar), author. | Sunstone Press.
Title: Hiking New Mexico's Chaco Canyon : the trails, the ruins, the history
    / James C. Wilson.
Other titles: Chaco Canyon : the trails, the ruins, the history | Hiking New
    Mexico
Description: Santa Fe, New Mexico : Sunstone Press, [2019] | Includes
    bibliographical references.
Identifiers: LCCN 2019023439 | ISBN 9781632932709 (Paperback)
    | ISBN 9781632933966 (Hardcover)
Subjects: LCSH: Hiking--New Mexico--Guidebooks. | Camping--New
    Mexico--Guidebooks. | Pueblo Indians--New Mexico--Chaco Culture National
    Historical Park. | Indians of North America--Four Corners Region. | Pueblo
    Bonito Site (N.M.)--Guidebooks. | Pueblo del Arroyo (New
    Mexico)--Guidebooks. | Day hiking--New Mexico--Guidebooks. | Walking--New
    Mexico--Guidebooks. | Backpacking--New Mexico--Guidebooks. | Rock
    climbing--New Mexico--Guidebooks. | Mountaineering--New
    Mexico--Guidebooks. | Historic sites--New Mexico--Guidebooks. |
    Trails--New Mexico--Guidebooks. | Natural history--New Mexico--Guidebooks.
    | New Mexico--Description and travel. | Four Corners Region--Description
    and travel. | New Mexico--Guidebooks. | Four Corners Region--Guidebooks.
Classification: LCC GV199.42.N6 W55 2019 | DDC 796.5109789--dc23
LC record available at https://lccn.loc.gov/2019023439

WWW.SUNSTONEPRESS.COM
SUNSTONE PRESS / POST OFFICE BOX 2321 / SANTA FE, NM 87504-2321 /USA
(505) 988-4418 / ORDERS ONLY (800) 243-5644 / FAX (505) 988-1025

Entry fees, campground fees and rules, as well as other rules regarding times and dates quoted here are based on information at the time of this book's publication and may change. Visitors to Chaco should check the Chaco Culture National Historical Park website for updated information.

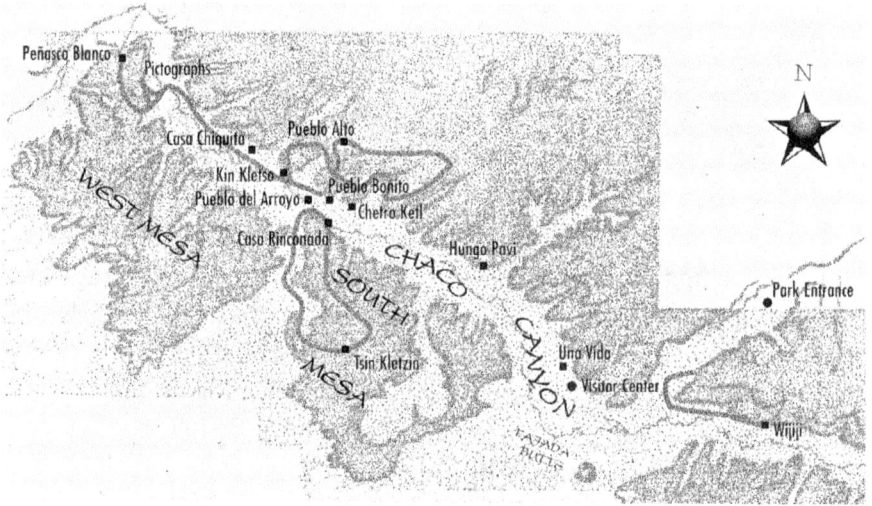

National Park Service map of Chaco Canyon.

Contents

PREFACE: HIKING WITH RESPECT

Chaco Culture National Historical Park is a UNESCO World Heritage Site. Please show respect when you hike at Chaco, not only because the Antiquities Act makes it a crime to destroy or steal antiquities, but because the Hopi, Zuni, Acoma and other Pueblos consider Chaco their ancestral homeland. The canyon is a sacred place, a spiritual center and symbol of migration valued by all New Mexicans. So please, don't destroy or deface any of the ruins or remove any objects from the park. Let's all commit to a humble, gentle way of being in the world and in doing so preserve our heritage.

Introduction: A Quick Overview of Chaco

Even though I've been hiking and camping at Chaco for over forty years, I can honestly say that on each excursion to the canyon I discover something new: a pictograph, a corner window, a stretch of ancient road, a new vista from the top of one of the mesas I had never before noticed. Why do I keep returning? Partly it's Chaco's rich history, as fascinating as it is mysterious. Partly it's the sheer rugged beauty of the canyon. And partly it's the spectacular ruins that have the timeless quality shared by other ancient ruins, the pyramids of Egypt or Machu Picchu, for example.

My friends tell me I'm a bit obsessed with Chaco because of my twice-yearly camping trips to the canyon. I would not disagree. I even set one of my mystery novels in Chaco. *Ghost Canyon*, the third of my Fernando Lopez Santa Fe Mystery Series, is set among the ruins and ghosts of Chaco Canyon. Where better to set a mystery?

To me, hiking in Chaco is like traveling back seven centuries to a time before the arrival of Europeans in the Americas. The trails take you through 1,200 years of Ancestral Puebloan history. You will walk on ancient roads, you will stand before ancient shrines and open kivas where religious ceremonies were performed by priests a thousand years ago. You will climb ancient stairways cut out of sheer sandstone cliffs up to mesas that provide panoramic views of the canyon's Great Houses and of the entire Four Corners area of Northwestern New Mexico.

Walking the trails you will come across the famous pictographs believed to be artistic representations of the 1054 supernova and of the 1066 appearance of Halley's Comet, as well as hundreds of other pictographs and petroglyphs of plants, animals, humans, and migration symbols. And you may, while hiking late in the afternoon or early evening, cross paths with the Chaco elk herd that comes down from South Mesa to feed along Chaco Wash. In short, you will hike the well-preserved remains of what was once the leading civilization of its time and place.

Yes, a thousand years ago greater Chaco was a bustling metropolis of roughly 20,000 inhabitants, with Great Houses and underground kivas built of sandstone masonry equal to anything built today. The Chacoans worked extensive fields, with dams and canals to irrigate their crops, including maize, beans, and squash. They built Great Kivas and large communal plazas for public functions as well as roads, some as wide as thirty feet, that extended out in every direction like tentacles reaching out to collect traders and nomadic hunter-gatherers from the Southern or Midwestern plains. Along the primary artery, the Great North Road, they built fire towers in a line-of-sight communication system that allowed them to communicate with northern outliers at places like Aztec Ruin, New Mexico, and Chimney Rock in Southern Colorado.

Chaco was an important trade center, where Ancestral Puebloans traded with Navajo, Ute, Apache, and other tribes from the North and East. Their trading partners extended West all the way to California and South to Mesoamerica, where they traded for cacao, macaws, sea shells, and other goods that were exotic to the desert Southwest. But Chaco was also an important ceremonial center, where religious ceremonies and rituals were performed throughout the year at times that were keyed to both the solar and lunar calendars.

Archaeologists believe the canyon has been occupied intermittently for up to 10,000 years. Several hundred years before Chaco emerged as an urban center, the inhabitants of the canyon lived in pit houses and were part of what is called the Basketmaker Culture. About 800 A.D. something dramatic occurred that enabled Chaco to become the preeminent regional power by about 900 AD. Possibly the transformative spark was provided by new building techniques imported from Mesoamerica, and/or the arrival of powerful clans that became the ruling elite of Chaco, sometimes called the *altepetl*.

Chaco's Great Houses tell the story. Construction of Pueblo Bonito, Penasco Blanco, and Una Vida began around 850. Chetro Ketl, Pueblo Alto, Hungo Pavi, and Casa Rinconada started about 1000–1027, Pueblo del Arroyo about 1075. The five other Great Houses were constructed in the first three decades of the 12th century: Wijiji, Tsin Kletsin, Kin Kletso, Casa Chiquita, and New Alto. By 1150 there were over thirty major outliers, Chaco-style Great Houses built in regional or satellite communities as far west as Canyon de Chelly, as far north as Chimney Rock, as far East as Pueblo Pintado, and as far south as Guadalupe Ruin.

The walls of the ancient buildings were built with sandstone mined from the cliffs of the canyon, chipped and fitted into place using a core-and-veneer construction, with the core being a mix of mud and rubble between the interior and exterior walls. The precision of the fitted stonework seems like a metaphor for the culture's interdependent relationship with the natural world. As the canyon developed into a metropolis and the Great Houses shot up to four and five stories, the walls got thicker, with wider cores, to support the additional weight. Upper level floors and roofs were composed of logs, branches, and mud.

This period of rapid growth lasted for some 300 years. Then, about 1150 or shortly thereafter, construction slowed to a stop at Chaco. Chaco's zenith, sometimes referred to as the Pax Chaco, lasted from 850 to about 1150 A.D. During the 1200s Chaco began losing population, gradually at first and then rapidly by the end of the century. By the early 1300s Chaco was nearly deserted, increasingly inhabited by nomadic groups who stayed for a short time and then moved on. By the end of the 14th century Chaco had become a city of ghosts.

So what happened? Several factors seem to have been involved in the depopulation of Chaco. First was a series of severe droughts culminating in the devastating drought of the last part of the 13th century that further damaged already depleted resources, including food and wood supplies. By 1300 the Chacoans had harvested virtually every tree in a 50-mile radius around the canyon. The scarcity of resources led in turn to civil strife and possible warfare with competing tribes from the Plains and other surrounding areas, although so far little evidence of violence at Chaco has been uncovered. Another contributing factor may have been the arrival of a new religion based on Kachinas that challenged the old elite and their priests who ruled by their knowledge of astronomical events. Or possibly Chacoans just grew tired of the hierarchical power structure at Chaco and decided to leave, either individually or with their clan, in search of a freer, more independent life. After all, migration for the Ancestral Puebloans (as their migration symbol implies) was a natural, ongoing process until they reached the "Center Place," which was different for different people and different groups.

In all likelihood the abandonment of Chaco was gradual, occurring over a century or so. The great diaspora saw many Chacoans migrate southeast to pueblos along the Rio Grande, from Taos Pueblo down to Isleta

Pueblo near Albuquerque. Others went north into southwestern Colorado and southeastern Utah. Still others went west into Arizona near Kayenta and the Hopi Mesas or southwest to Zuni, Acoma, and Laguna. They left behind a city of stone that has survived, deserted, for more than 700 years.

Today, getting to Chaco Canyon is not an easy task. Chaco is not a roadside stop or a quick photo op. I'm talking about a 3-4 hour drive from Santa Fe, and a 2-3 hour drive from Albuquerque, depending on road conditions. The turn-off to the canyon is on Highway 550 near Nageezi, which is halfway between Cuba and Aztec, New Mexico. You take County Road 7900 South, then turn right on 7950, and drive a total of 16 miles, most of it unpaved. The unpaved portion is deeply rutted and especially dangerous in inclement weather, when an all-wheel-drive vehicle is recommended if not required. From Durango to the north, Chaco is a two-hour drive south on 550, a distance of about 100 miles.

Entering the canyon you will see majestic Fajada Butte off to the left and then the Gallo Campground on the right. The Visitor Center is about a mile further on the right, where permits to enter the canyon can be purchased. Permits cost anywhere from $15 for an individual to $25 for a vehicle containing multiple passengers. The permits are good for seven days. Senior and Access passes are honored. The canyon is open from 7 a.m. to sunset daily. At sunset the entrance gate on the 8-mile Chaco Loop is closed and locked, so be sure you're out by sunset or you may end up spending the night with the ghosts of Chaco. The park is closed on Thanksgiving, Christmas Eve, Christmas Day, New Year's Eve, and New Years Day.

Now to the trails.

Good hiking.

What to Know, What to Bring

Chaco Canyon presents what I would call a challenging environment, smoking hot in summer and bitterly cold in winter. So you need to prepare carefully, whether hiking or camping. First, keep in mind there are no services in the canyon: no gas stations, no convenience stores, and no restaurants. That means you need to have plenty of gas when you arrive and carry whatever food and supplies you will need during your stay. Gas can be especially tricky because even though the dot-on-the-map Nageezi, where you turn off to Chaco, does have a gas station, it's not always open. To get to the closest gas station after Nageezi, you have to drive another hour or so. I always make sure to arrive with at least a half tank of gas in my Subaru because the long road into the canyon burns a good deal of gas as does driving around the 8-mile Chaco loop that takes you to the various ruins and trails. The loop is one-way, except for a short portion that takes you to the Pueblo del Arroyo Parking Lot.

Bring food, lots of it. Hiking around the canyon and climbing cliff trails burns up calories fast. You'll need to replenish your fuel frequently. I bring food supplies for meals and lots of healthy snacks for instant energy on the hiking trails: nuts and fruit mostly. Make sure you bring a camp stove of choice with you, because even though there are metal fire pits with grates at each campsite, the Four Corners area of the Southwest has been bone dry in recent years, constantly in a state of drought, and often you will not be allowed to build a campfire at Chaco. And keep your eyes open for notices. On my most recent camping trip to Chaco, just a few months ago, we somehow missed the "No Fires Allowed" sign and found ourselves reprimanded by a park ranger. Ignorance is no excuse, I discovered.

I always bring lots of water to Chaco. When I camp, I fill a five-gallon water cooler for drinking, cooking, and washing. Remember, the hotter it is, the more water you drink. And you can count on Chaco being hot, at least from mid-May through the end of October, and I mean very hot, especially when you're hiking the longer trails or climbing cliffs. The water at the Visitor Center is listed as potable, but not the water in the campground, so you have to be careful. I've always found it easier to bring my own, which I know is safe.

Bring lots of sunscreen, as well as sun gear, hats and high SPF clothing. Just as important is a pair of serious hiking boots. Remember, you will be hiking over extremely rough terrain, climbing on rocks and across sandy arroyos. Every so often I encounter a couple of young hikers trying to negotiate a difficult trail wearing flip-flops. I kid you not. I even saw two people last year trying to make it down the White House Trail into Canyon de Chelly stopping every few feet to adjust their flip-flops and remove rocks. This is hiking insanity! Protect your feet. Wear heavy duty hiking boots.

I also bring a compass, because I like to check the astronomical orientation of the ruins. A compass also allows you to check your exact location in relation to the ruins, and the trail, at all times. You don't have to worry much about rain gear, because it rarely rains at Chaco, but I always throw in a poncho just to be on the safe side. A poncho also comes in handy if the wind kicks up, a frequent occurrence in the Southwest. In addition to all that, I bring my usual camping gear that I would bring on any camping trip. Remember, though, that while Chaco is very hot during the summer months, it is also very cold at night during the winter months and even the transitional months of May and November. Average high and low temperatures for May are 77 and 45. For November the averages drop to 54 for the high and 27 for the low. The average lows for April and October are 36 and 38 respectively. So during these transitional months, you need to bring warm night clothing, a warm sleeping bag, and a sturdy tent.

I'm happy to report that you don't have to worry about bringing a portable toilet, since there are good facilities at the Gallo Campground, at the Visitor Center, and at many of the trailheads. The Gallo Campground has sinks, but no showers.

One other thing I always bring with me to Chaco is hand sanitizer and soap. Not than I'm a germaphobe, far from it. The reason I bring a supply of soaps is that hanta virus and plague are present in the Southwest and can be spread by the fleas found on rodents, and yes you will find an occasional furry little creature scurrying around your campsite. They may look cute, but the parasites they carry can be dangerous. Avoid feeding or encouraging them. You may also want to consider insect repellent, even though there are virtually no flying insects at Chaco because of the dry climate. Better to be safe than sorry.

Most problematic, especially for millenials: there is no cell service at Chaco. None. Some people find it unbearable when they can't check their phone every few minutes or post selfies on Facebook whenever a photo op occurs. Not me. I find it liberating to be free from the nuisance of social media for two or three days. In case of emergency, you can always use the land line available at the Visitor Center. Otherwise, why not enjoy yourself for a few short hours or days without the constant beeping, dinging, and ringing of your cell phone? Let's kick back and enjoy the quiet. We'll be back on the phone soon enough.

Given all the above, is Chaco appropriate for the entire family? Maybe. To be honest, I don't see many children under the age of 13 at Chaco. I think this is partly because of the climate and partly because there are few child-friendly amenities in the canyon. Again, you can count on Chaco being extremely hot in the summer and even in transitional months like May and October. Also, there's no playground, swimming pool, or wi-fi to keep kids entertained. Only hiking, which itself can be a problem for some family members.

The Downtown Chaco attractions, meaning primarily Pueblo Bonito and Chetro Ketl, are easily accessible to nearly everyone, including children, seniors, and most people with disabilities. So, too, is the walk to Pueblo del Arroyo from its parking lot, as is the short walk to Una Vida from the Visitor Center. However, the longer trails that involve climbing are much more difficult. Keep in mind that Chaco's elevation is 6,200 feet, which can be a problem for hikers who are not used to the altitude, especially when climbing. So I would only recommend the North, West, and South Mesa trails for experienced hikers who have the fitness and stamina to climb rocky terrain and survive hikes of five to ten miles. For a more moderate hike, you might consider the trail to Wijiji, which is flat and involves no climbing.

What about the family pet? Do you take Fido with you, or do you leave the dog at home? To me it makes sense to leave the dog at home. Why? Because dogs are not allowed on the ruins, so if you do bring your pet, you'll have to figure out what to do with it while you hike. And remember, Chaco is unforgivingly hot with little shade for humans or animals.

The view as you approach Pueblo Bonito.

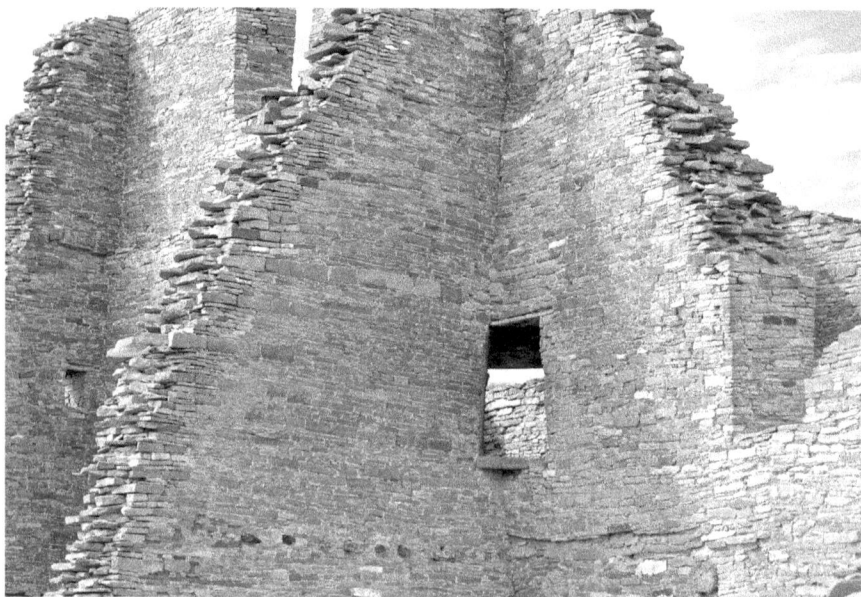
The view as you approach Pueblo Bonito.

TRAIL 1: DOWNTOWN CHACO: PUEBLO BONITO AND CHETRO KETL

One mile loop from the Pueblo Bonito parking lot, approximately 2 hours with stops.

 You probably want to start with Chaco's main attractions, Pueblo Bonito and Chetro Ketl, located close together in the center of the canyon. Both can be accessed from the Bonito parking lot. Follow the trail west and watch Bonito (Spanish for "Beautiful Town") seem to rise up out of the canyon floor as you come closer. You first notice the intricate masonry of the sandstone walls, jagged shapes against a deep blue sky. The corner windows/doors stand out, positioned to look southeast toward where the sun would rise over the horizon on the winter solstice. In its earliest configuration Bonito had a solstitial orientation; that changed sometime after 1085 when a north-south wall was built splitting its main plaza and realigning the great house to a north-south orientation. Did the realignment reflect a power struggle between competing clans or competing religions? Some archaeologists think so.

 As the trail slopes up to the base of the cliff behind Bonito you begin to see the enormity of the ruin: 650 rooms, most of them rectangular, and forty round kivas, built in the D-shaped configuration common to Puebloan Great Houses. Most of the rooms were used for storage of supplies or trade goods, or possibly as spaces to accommodate traders and pilgrims passing through Chaco. The families or clans who occupied Bonito lived in the smaller kivas. The large or Great Kivas were reserved for public ceremonies or spectacles. The pile of sandstone boulders you're standing on was once a large vertical section of the cliff known as Threatening Rock. Chacoans had propped it up centuries ago with makeshift supporting walls of mud and stone, but the rock collapsed finally in January 1941, falling onto the Great

House and destroying part of the rear wall and about thirty rooms.

Descending into the first of the two main plazas in the center of the ruin, you get the feel of what it must have been like to live in Bonito, of the monumental architecture that surrounds you. At its zenith the rear portion of Bonito was four and five stories high, as high as Taos Pueblo is today. The architecture is as much for spectacle as it is for residential purposes.

The trail takes you down to a lower, underground level of maze-like rooms adjoined by small, T-shaped doors, a trademark of Chaco. The doors are very small, so my guess is that the enlarged top of the T allowed Chacoans to more easily carry loads of wood or goods for trade or storage from one room to another. Notice, also, more corner windows at the top of the walls, which get narrower as they shoot upward. The circular holes about head high were sockets for the wooden beams that once supported the ceiling above your head.

Again, the Chacoans built their dwellings with sandstone from the surrounding cliffs. The walls are built in what's called core-and-veneer construction, where a core of rubble and mud fills the space between two walls of chipped and fitted stones. Lower level floors have thicker cores so as to hold the weight of the floors and roofs above. There are four types of veneer stone, I through IV, with I being the most primitive and used in older

Lower rooms in Pueblo Bonito.

construction. Types II, III, and IV came later and involve more of a pattern in the stones used, with repeating bands of small and large stones, almost like a rug or basket weaving. McElmo was the last type, with a rougher looking front that looks similar to brick. Most of the Great Houses are a mix of types, relating to different stages of development. Types III and IV are the most intricate.

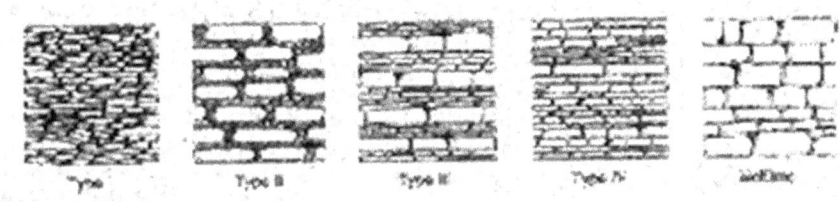

Core-and-veneer masonry types at Bonito from Type I, the earliest, to McElmo, the latest.

Take the trail back up to the plaza areas and follow the north-south wall to the rear of Bonito. Step outside and you see the enormous back wall of Bonito along the base of North Mesa. The wall, once plumb, has required the support of buttresses to remain intact since the collapse of Threatening Rock. You will also notice round indentations along the cliff face of North Mesa, where Ancestral Puebloans build small room blocks against the cliff.

Stop near the large modern buttress holding up the wall and notice the nearby doorway and niches in the rear wall. Here was where Richard Wetherill, the first (amateur) archaeologist to excavate Pueblo Bonito, built his first trading post in 1897, from where he sold many of the precious artifacts recovered from the ruin. The Bonito Trading Post was a small stone structure built out from the rear wall of the Great House. For more space, Wetherill opened up the massive rear wall to provide access to three or four rooms in Bonito, which became part of his original trading post.

Now walk west around the curved D to the northwest corner of the ruin and stop. You are standing before the oldest part of Bonito, built between 850 and 900 (all dates included in this book were established by dendrochronology, or tree ring dating). You will notice the primitive Type I masonry of the small rooms in this famous suite. Why is it famous? Because here in Room 33 a National Geographic Expedition under the direction of Neil M. Judd in 1921 discovered fourteen burials of individuals believed to have been Chaco's ruling elite. Buried with the fourteen individuals were tens of thousands of turquoise beads and pendants—more than 80 percent of all turquoise found in Chaco—as well as large quantities of shell and jet, flutes, ceremonial staffs, cylindrical jars, and conch shell trumpets. A total of more than 30,000 artifacts were recorded and catalogued by the National Geographic team.

But the treasure wasn't confined to Room 33. Next door in Room 28 archaeologists discovered 111 cylindrical jars with traces of cacao from Mesoamerica.

So these fourteen individuals were clearly very rich and very powerful. What makes this story even more interesting is that recent researchers have carbon-dated and analyzed the DNA of the fourteen bodies preserved at the American Museum of Natural History in New York. They dated the bodies from 800 to 1130, and they discovered that nine of the fourteen individuals shared the exact mitochondrial DNA, which can only be passed through the mother. The oldest, or "lineage founder" as they refer to Burial #14, was female and was buried with the most jewelry and ceremonial paraphernalia.

All this suggests that power at Chaco was hierarchical, belonged to this small group of people, and was passed down through a female line

Here in the northwest suite of rooms, the oldest part of Bonito, was where fourteen bodies of Chaco royalty and 111 jars with traces of cacao were discovered.

between 800 and 1130 A.D. In other words, Chaco was hierarchical and matrilineal, according to these researchers, led by Douglas J. Kennett, an archaeologist at Penn State University. Kennett points out that matrilineal social systems are common in the Pueblo Southwest (in the Western Pueblos of Hopi, Zuni, Acoma, Laguna, as well as the Keresan-speaking Rio Grande Pueblos of Cochiti, San Felipe, Santo Domingo, and Zia).

In passing, let me just say that the matrilineal part of Kennett's theory is not universally accepted, even though the facts would seem to support his argument.

When you finish with Chaco Royalty, follow the trail around to the front of Bonito. Back in the early 1970s, when I first started coming to Chaco, you could park anywhere in front of Bonito, wander around the ruin and along Chaco Wash without restrictions. You rarely saw another hiker. Also back then, all the ruins were littered with the famous black-and-white Chaco pottery fragments. The shards were literally everywhere, strewn about the midden trash mounds and scattered about the trails and across the mesas. Today you can walk for hours without seeing a single shard. Sadly, selfish visitors have picked the canyon clean, eager to have a souvenir from Chaco. I say sadly, because this theft of time diminishes the experience of all those who come after. To me, nothing evokes the lived life of an ancient culture more than these colorful artifacts. That's why we go to museums—to get a glimpse of all that's been removed, looted, or stolen from places like Chaco.

Enough ruminating on the past! Forget the good old days of unfettered hiking. Returning to the here and now, you can step inside one of the front doorways and explore the main plaza, kivas and all. The plazas were public spaces, like today's town squares, where public events took place. Dances, processions, and especially trade fairs would have been held frequently on the plaza. Chaco was, after all, a major trading station on trade routes to California and Mesoamerica. And the fairs attracted more regional trading partners such as the Navajo, Ute, Apache, and many of the midwestern tribes.

When you're finished with the plazas, make your way around to the northeast corner of Bonito where, at the base of the North Mesa cliff, you will find a narrow trail leading east to Chetro Ketl, a short distance away. On the trail you will see petroglyphs and more pecked holes in the cliff, where beams once supported one or two-story structures built out from the cliff.

There is also a trail to Chetro Ketl from the Bonito parking lot, but I prefer the cliff trail because it takes you directly to the magnificent rear wall of Chetro Ketl. To my eye, the wall is pretty darn close to being perfectly plumb after one thousand years, an incredible feat of engineering. The longest, straightest part of the wall extends a good 450 feet. You can measure it yourself!

Construction of Chetro Ketl (which may be a rough translation of a Navajo word meaning "Rain Pueblo") began around the year 1000, considerably later than Bonito. By about 1100, when the building stopped, Chetro Ketl included some 500 rooms in the typical D-shaped configuration, about 225 on the first level and 275 on the second and third levels. At 5.7

The rear wall of Chetro Ketl seen from above.

acres, it has the largest surface area of any of Chaco's Great Houses. Edgar Hewett of the School of American Research excavated Chetro Ketl in 1920. Like Bonito, Chetro Ketl was built with a southeast alignment, oriented to either the winter solstice or, more likely, the lunar minor standstill, according to the findings of the Chaco Solstice Project.

This brings me to the relatively new field of archaeoastronomy. Researchers have found that the major Great Houses at Chaco are oriented to either solar or lunar cycles. Most readers understand solar orientations:

a southeast winter solstice alignment, or a north-south Cardinal alignment, for example. Lunar cycles, and lunar orientations to the minor standstill and the major standstill are far more complex. Anna Sofaer, director of the Chaco Solstice Project, explains that each month the moon shifts from rising roughly in the northeast to rising roughly in the southeast and from setting roughly in the northwest to setting roughly in the southwest, but if we look closer we see that the envelope of these excursions expands and contracts through the 18.6-year standstill cycle. A major standstill occurs when this envelope is at its maximum width, whereas a minor standstill occurs when the envelope is at its minimum width. A minor standstill occurs 9.3 years later than a major standstill. During a standstill, the moon seems to 'stand still', just as the sun does when it reaches solstice. Complicated stuff, so for a more thorough explanation, with diagrams and photos, see Anna Sofaer's *Chaco Astronomy: An Ancient American Cosmology* and J. McKim Malville's *Guide to Prehistoric Astronomy in the Southwest*. Terrific books, both of them.

Anyway, unlike Bonito, Chetro Ketl was never realigned to a Cardinal or north-south orientation. I've always wondered: did the two Great Houses compete with each other? Was there friction or outright hostility? They lived side by side, the two largest, most powerful Great Houses in the canyon controlled, one supposes, by different clans. From our perspective today, after a century of constant warfare, it's hard to imagine the two pueblos were able to exist in such close proximity without problems. I mean, here in the 21st century we're lucky if anyone can get along with anyone else! Could friction between the two Great Houses have hastened the end of the Pax Chaco? We may never know.

If you follow the trail back around to the front of Chetro Ketl, you will come across another engineering marvel, literally. You will be walking across a main plaza that is considerably higher than the canyon below. In fact, the Chacoans built the elevated platform a good twelve feet above the canyon floor using tons of soil and rock hauled by hand. The elevated plaza is unique to Chetro Ketl. Its purpose is believed to be practical: to avoid flooding from the seasonal waterfalls that come pouring down from deep ravines in the North Mesa directly behind the Great House. Which, in turn, gives credence to the to the theory that the name Chetro Ketl comes from the Navajo word for "Rain Pueblo."

Off to your left you will see a glass door behind which is the upper story of a multi-storied room block that contains original floor and roofing sections You can view an actual example of how the Chacoans constructed their floors and roofs by using ponderosa pine beams (or vigas) covered with willow branches and then plastered with layers of juniper bark and mud. The Chacoans used an estimated 26,000 trees from forests as far as fifty miles away in the construction of Chetro Ketl. Around 200,000 trees total were used in the construction of all the Great Houses in the canyon. You will also notice a decorative mural on the east wall of this room, a blue and green design that appears to be steps going up and down.

To the east, the front of the Great House presents another feature unique to Chetro Ketl, Colonnade Architecture. Known for its columns, this architecture was common in the Toltec culture of Central Mexico (about 700–1000) but doesn't exist anywhere else in Chaco or its outliers. You can't help but notice the long, narrow room at the front of the ruin with its row of columns looking out on the plaza area. Apparently the columns were added around 1100, late in the construction of Chetro Ketl. Mesoamerican influence? The answer would seem to be yes, given the presence in Chaco of Macaws, cacao, sea shells, and precious stones from Mexico and Central America.

Straight ahead you come to the Great Kiva of Chetro Ketl, the second

Mesoamerican Colonnade Architecture at Chetro Ketl.

largest Great Kiva in Chaco. Only Casa Rinconada is larger. The kiva was built on top of an earlier structure, apparently an older kiva. As we'll see when we get to Casa Rinconada, Great Kivas contain the same formalized features, including an entryway and antechamber on the plaza level, a low stone bench encircling the room, and a raised fire box and floor vaults for storage, presumably of ceremonial costumes and other paraphernalia.

As you make your way around the eastern wall to the rear of the ruin, you see what's called an elevated kiva built within a rectangular room, adding more walls, more security for its inhabitants. Notice, also, the balconies built on the rear wall that look out on the box canyon to the northeast of the ruin. Here is where Chetro Ketl's midden, or trash mound, was located, as well as their agricultural fields, which were irrigated primarily by rain water draining down from the canyon walls. If you look closely, you might also see the remains of Lizard House, a small ruin built against the cliff east of Chetro Ketl. Behind the ruin is a small cave in the cliff used by the Ancestral Puebloans.

As you head west, back toward the parking lot, notice the crevice in the cliff. If you look closely, you will see faint steps carved into the sandstone and small holes, or handholds, along the sides of the stairs. This stairway allowed Chacoans to climb to the top of North Mesa where one of the many

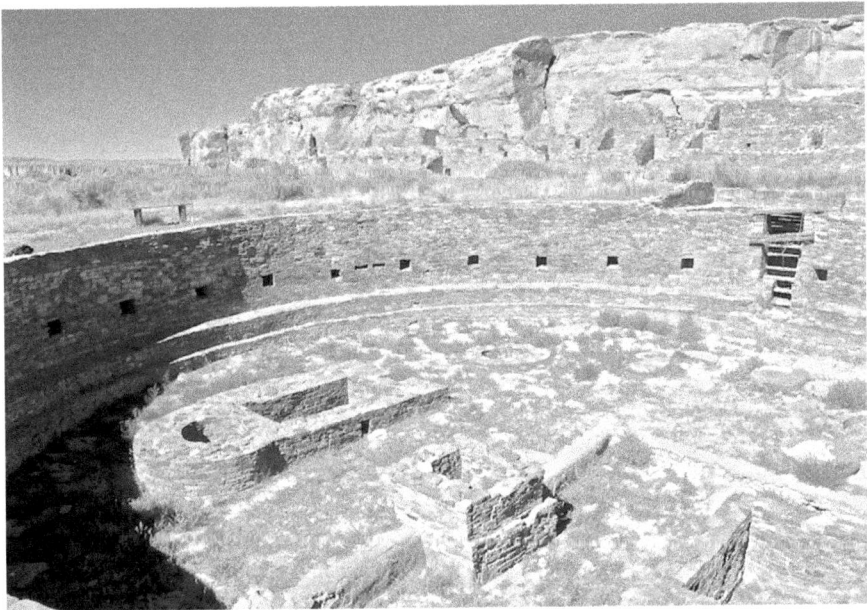

Chetro Ketl's Great Kiva.

ancient roads led from Chetro Ketl to Pueblo Alto, three-quarters of a mile away.

Time for a break? You can sit on the bench along the rear wall of Chetro Ketl and enjoy the view of the box canyon behind the ruin and the towering cliffs overhead. Or you can do what I do. I generally tour Pueblo Bonito and Chetro Ketl in the morning, which you can do easily in two hours, then drive down to the Pueblo del Arroyo parking lot. The shaded picnic tables at the end of the parking lot provide an ideal place for lunch or just refreshments if you're pressed for time. From there, you can follow the trail up to Pueblo Alto on North Mesa, or you can continue west to Penasco Blanco on West Mesa, your choice. Let's do North Mesa first.

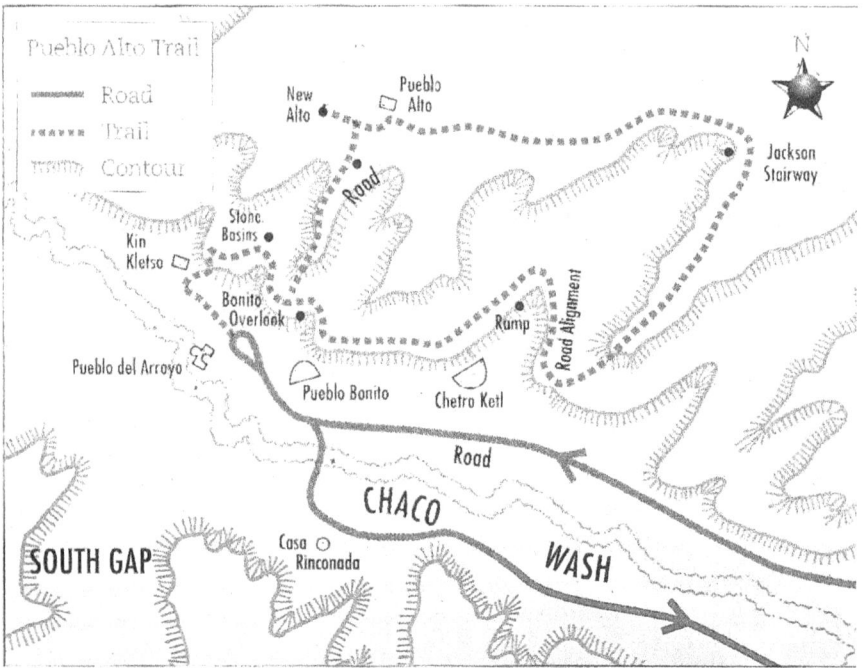

National Park Service Map of North Mesa.

Chacoan stairway to North Mesa.

Kin Kletso from North Mesa.

Trail 2: North Mesa: Kin Kletso, Pueblo Alto, New Alto, and Jackson Stairway

5.1 miles from the Pueblo del Arroyo parking lot at the western end of the Chaco Loop, 5 hours.

For a shorter hike, you can do the first leg from Kin Kletso to Pueblo Alto and New Alto, 3.2 miles, 3 hours.

From the Pueblo del Arroyo parking lot it's a short walk to Kin Kletso (Navajo for "Yellow House"). It's a small rectangular Great House of only sixty-five rooms, including five kivas, with McElmo style masonry. The ruin was first excavated in 1934 by Edwin Ferdon as part of a team sponsored by the University of New Mexico and the School of American Research. Like Chetro Ketl, Kin Kletso has a southeastern alignment, possibly oriented to the lunar minor standstill. The ruin does not have a Great Kiva or plaza, but it does have a tower kiva at the west end. More important to hikers, it's where we catch the ancient Chacoan stairway up to North Mesa.

You have to look carefully. The stairway, directly behind Kin Kletso, is easy to miss. You first see a narrow ribbon of a trail that seems to disappear in a stand of boulders, but on second glance you see the boulders are stepping stones up the lower half of the cliff. Then the trail reappears as a series of steps cut out of the soft sandstone that take you up between a narrow gap in the cliff. This can be tricky because the steps are steep and if you're carrying a heavy backpack, as I usually am, you can easily fall backward. This happened to me my last time up to North Mesa. To prevent a falling domino effect, it's safer when climbers spread out and put some distance between each other. Fortunately the gap in the cliff is narrow, so that you can hold on to both sides if you find yourself slipping. As long as you're not sandwiched between two other climbers.

When you step out on top of North Mesa into bright sunshine, you'll see the entire canyon spread out below. Even if you've lived in the Southwest

Pueblo Bonito overlook.

for many years, you will appreciate the clarity of light in New Mexico, the clarity that has attracted Georgia O'Keeffe and hundreds of other visual artists over the years.

The trail on top of North Mesa is clearly designated by cairns and occasional wooden signs. It takes you east along the cliff, passing by a series of sea fossils from when Chaco was under water during the Cretaceous Period, past pecked basins that were used by the Chacoans as receptacles for offerings, and past stone circles used for ancient ceremonies. After about a mile you will find yourself approaching the Pueblo Bonito overlook, a great place to take photos of Bonito. Viewed from above, you see the enormity of the ruin, the geometrical patters of the rooms and kivas, and the straight north-south wall cutting through the center of Bonito. Be careful, though. Don't get too close to the canyon rim. Much of the rock is loose or splitting from the cliff.

When you finish snapping photos, you return to the trail and head due north on the remnants of the Great North Road. Segments of this road, the Chacoan version of a freeway, are thirty feet wide. Eventually you will come to a sign marking another Chacoan stairway, where the steps are carved out of the sandstone ridge. Once you get beyond this ridge, Pueblo Alto is clearly visible on the northern horizon, straight ahead. A smaller ruin, New Alto, is visible about 200 yards to the left of Alto.

If you're pressed for time, or feeling lazy, you may want to skip New

New Alto.

Alto, a small square-shaped ruin similar to Casa Chiquita in the canyon proper. Alto means "High Town" in Spanish, so obviously New Alto means "New High Town." It contains fifty-eight one- and two-story rooms built around a single kiva, with typical late occupation McElmo masonry. Like Alto, it has a cardinal or north-south orientation, but unlike Alto and most of the other Great Houses, it has never been excavated.

However, you don't want to skip Pueblo Alto, primarily because of its location on the Great North Road. As the northernmost Great House in the canyon, the Great North Road extends from Alto all the way to Kurtz Canyon and possibly beyond to Salmon Ruins and Aztec Ruins. Fire towers have been discovered along the Great North Road that would enable a line-of-sight communication system to connect with northern outliers in places as distant as Chimney Rock, Colorado, near Pagosa Springs. Not only the Great North Road, but a maze of ancient roads branch out in pretty much every direction from Alto. The ancient roads have been mapped by means of aerial photography and, more recently, by lidar, and can be viewed online with a simple Google search.

In fact, Pueblo Alto was the center of a complex or community of dwellings on the North Mesa that included six separate structures within a 200 yard radius from Alto. These six late, McElmo ruins include Rabbit Run and East Ruin. Though small, the six ruins had an estimated 200 plus rooms combined. The purpose of these smaller 'outbuildings' is a matter of some dispute. Some may have been farming outposts, since there are a series of

Pueblo Alto.

basins and artificial berms near the ruins. Some may have been watch or guard posts, monitoring approaching traffic on the Great North Road. Some may have been guest houses for arriving pilgrims or traders. Who knows?

The high density of ancient roads around Pueblo Also indicates its importance as a communication/transportation center linking the Great Houses in the canyon below to distant Great Houses to the north. In all, there may be as many as seventy ancient road fragments at Chaco, according to John Roney (see suggested reading). Only fourteen of these fragments were longer than 3.0 kilometers. Mysteriously, some of the road fragments are parallel, and some have as many as four parallel tracks, suggesting they were used for ceremonial processions or spectacles. What's apparent is that the roads were not only physical, they were symbolic and metaphorical as well. They provided the web that connected Great Houses with both landscape and Chacoan astronomy. I quote grand theoretician Stephen H. Lekson in *The Chaco Meridian*: "The purpose of the roads formally entering a Great House was to anchor that place in spiritual space and to serve as a portal between worlds. Roads acted as reminders of a common belief system that held Chaco culture together" (xv).

Pueblo Alto has a classic D-shaped configuration, with a north-south orientation. In fact, Alto is on a north-south line that bisects the canyon from Alto on North Mesa to Tsin Kletzin on South Mesa. Pueblo Bonito is only a few degrees west of this line, which is about 108 degrees longitude. Stephen H. Lekson calls this line the "Chaco Meridian." Lekson argues in his

Chaco's Great North Road.

book of the same name that the line had deep significance to the Chacoans, and when they abandoned Chaco, they moved first north to Aztec Ruins in northern New Mexico and later south to Pacquime in northern Mexico, always following the meridian.

At any rate, Pueblo Alto has 130 rooms and eighteen kivas built in mixed masonry styles. It was excavated relatively recently by the National Park Service's Chaco Project, 1976–1978. Though typical in most respects, Pueblo Alto has two distinct features that make it unique among Chacoan Great Houses: the entire ruin was only one story high, and it did not have a Great Kiva. The rooms appeared to have been used for storage and/or by visitors who traveled to Chaco for feasts, trade fairs, or religious ceremonies. The Chaco Project discovered vast amounts of broken pottery shards and animal bones in a huge trash midden east of the ruin, what researchers believe are the remains of widespread public events at Alto. The rooms show little evidence of long-term residential use.

At this point in my North Mesa hike I like to stop and take at least a water break. Conveniently, the walls of Pueblo Alto provide ample shade for a bit of a rest. I'll stop here for a snack, or to eat a quick lunch, and to readjust my camera equipment. The views from the North Mesa Trail from this point on are spectacular, but distant, so I usually change camera lenses here, mounting my longest zoom lens.

After touring Alto, you have several choices. First choice: you can call it quits, turn around, and head back to Kin Kletso and the parking lot. Second choice: you can hike north a few hundred feet to another very

Pueblo Alto wall.

small ruin, Rabbit Run, which is on the park maps but marginally off limits. There's not much left of Rabbit Run, but looking north from the ruin you do get a sense of how expansive the Chacoan road system must have been in this vast landscape. Third choice: you can continue east on the main trail to the Jackson Stairway and circle around to Kin Kletso and the parking lot, the full five-hour hike.

Rabbit Run and sentinel.

When I'm not continuing on to the Jackson Stairway, I will at least take another look at Rabbit Run, about 100 yards north of Alto. This is a very small, unexcavated ruin on the Great North Road. On my last visit I discovered Rabbit Run wasn't entirely abandoned. When I went to step over the front wall into the ruin, I spotted a large snake just inside the wall, guarding the ruin. Yikes! I snapped my foot back and caught my breath. My hike had almost come to an abrupt end. In retrospect, I have to give the snake credit: he was just doing his job, keeping people off and out of the ruin. My bad.

Anyway, if you continue hiking east you'll come across yet another small ruin called simply East Ruin. Again, there's not much to look at here, just some crumbled wall fragments. But the view from the trail as you approach Jackson Stairway and then circle around to the Chetro Ketl overlook is nothing short of spectacular. You can see several of Chaco's Great Houses and the vast panorama of mountain ranges and buttes surrounding the canyon.

After East Ruin the trail continues due east along the mesa top for about two miles and then turns to the southwest. As you approach the turn you will see the Jackson Stairway at the northeast corner of the canyon. The stairway was named for Willam Henry Jackson, a photographer with the 1877 U.S. Geological Survey. The steps, carved out of the sandstone ridge in two banks, at one time provided access to Chetro Ketl below. Today they are fragile and strictly off limits.

From there the trail heads southwest on the mesa and then loops around the head of the canyon to the north, passing another Chacoan road segment. The rocks off to the left of the trail are the remains of masonry curbing constructed along the sides of the road. The trail then heads north again and loops around the box canyon behind Chetro Ketl to the Chetro Ketl Overlook. Along the way you will see a ramp on the northwestern corner of the box canyon. Built with tons of dirt and rock, the ramp extends more than halfway up to the top of the mesa, once providing access to the maze of Chacoan roads on North Mesa. From a distance the ramp looks like the result of a mudslide or collapsed cliff, but if you look closely you will find the remnants of masonry walls that stabilized the mound, built by the Chacoans as part of their road system.

Once you reach the Chetro Ketl Overlook, you owe it to yourself to take a break. Not only have you hiked over four miles of rough terrain, you've come to another great place for photographs. Looking down on the Great House you get a better sense of the magnificence of its defining features than you can from below. I mean, of course, its rear wall, its Great Kiva, and its raised plaza. But be careful. The cliffs are just as perilous as those overlooking Pueblo Bonito.

If you survive the Chetro Ketl overlook and the 5.1-mile hike, then simply follow the trail back to the ancient stairway at Kin Kletso and down to the Pueblo del Arroyo parking lot. Once there, you can enjoy the shaded picnic tables or head back to Gallo to set up camp.

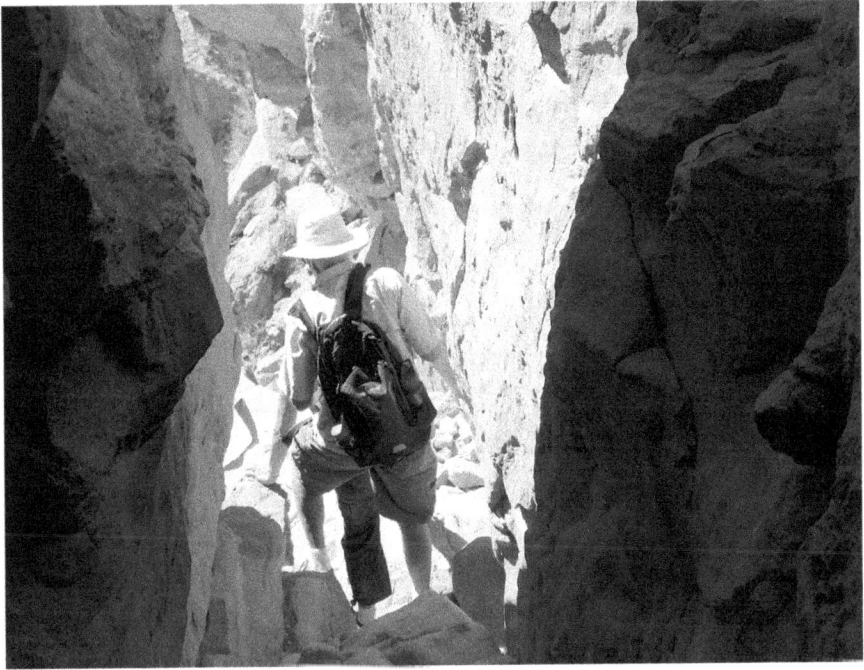

The author climbing down the ancient stairway. (Courtesy of Roger McNew)

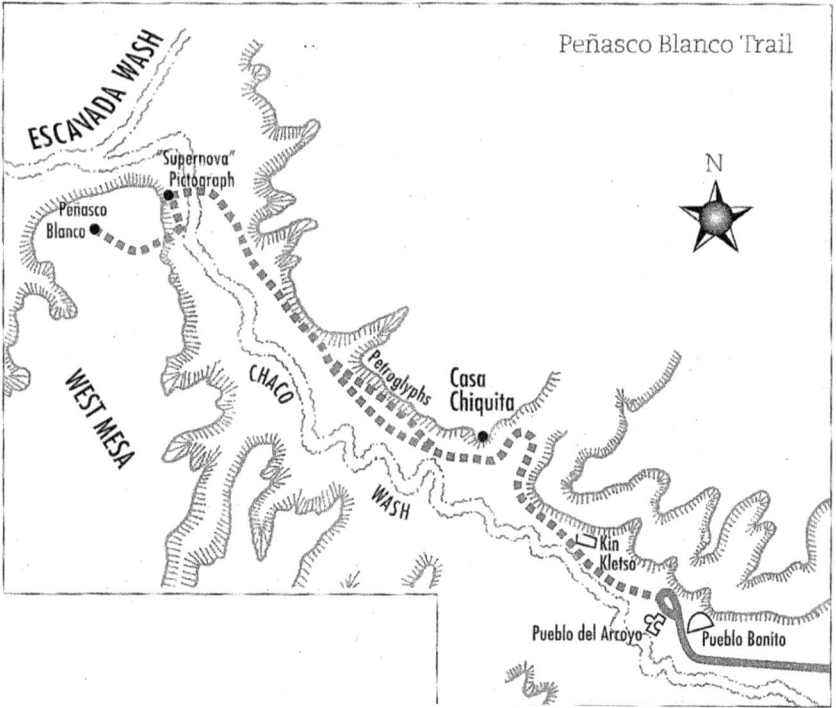

National Park Service Map of West Mesa.

TRAIL 3: WEST MESA: PUEBLO DEL ARROYO, CASA CHIQUITA, PENASCO BLANCO, ASTRONOMICAL PICTOGRAPHS, AND THE CONVERGENCE OF THE CHACO AND ESCAVADA WASHES

7.2 miles, 6 hours from the Pueblo del Arroyo parking lot.

The trail to Penasco Blanco on the West Mesa also begins at the Pueblo del Arroyo parking lot. If you haven't done it already, you can combine a quick look at Pueblo del Arroyo, a short walk southeast from the parking

Pueblo del Arroyo.

lot, with the longer, more difficult hike to the top of West Mesa. The West Mesa trail is the longest and to me the most difficult of the Chaco trails, not because it involves strenuous climbing, which it does, but because it offers so many side attractions that can seriously extend the time it takes to finish the hike. If you're like me, you can get easily sidetracked by a pictograph, a small, unnamed ruin, or even a box canyon that promises a spectacular view.

Warning: try to limit your side excursions or you may find yourself on an all-day hike on West Mesa.

Let's start with Pueblo del Arroyo, next door to the parking lot. This large ruin is unique because it's the only Great House in the interior of the canyon not backed up against the North Mesa. The Chacoans built it alongside Chaco Wash, far from any cliff. Why? Well, for one thing Pueblo del Arroyo offers a direct view through South Gap, which would allow them to monitor the ancient roads that entered the canyon from the south. Also, being next to the wash was an ideal location for water and irrigation control, a necessity for tending the fields planted on the floor of the canyon.

A classic D-shaped Great House, Pueblo del Arroyo has a southeast alignment, oriented to either the winter solstice or the lunar minor standstill. It's a large ruin, the fourth largest at Chaco, with about 300 rooms and 17 kivas in what was once a four-story structure. As you walk through the ruin you will notice partial tri-walls, which were added in the 1100s, more than a century after construction on Pueblo del Arroyo began. These are the only tri-walls in Chaco Canyon. You will see more tri-walls at Aztec Ruins, when we get to Chaco outliers. The Great House was first excavated by Neil M. Judd 1923–1927 for the National Geographic Society.

When you're finished, return to the Pueblo del Arroyo parking lot and then follow the trail west past Kin Kletso. You will be walking on an historic Navajo wagon road that runs alongside Chaco Wash. The road was used by the Navajo and later by Spanish and Anglo traders in the late 19th and early 20th centuries. At one time the road led to the Tsaya Trading Post near Lake Valley and north to the Hatch Brothers Trading Post at Waterflow west of Farmington. Richard Wetherill used the road to ship freight when he excavated Pueblo Bonito and later when he operated his Pueblo Bonito Trading Post in the canyon.

Soon the trail juts to the right and loops a box canyon, where you might notice, if you look closely, the remnants of NM Route 57, which was the previous entrance to the canyon from the north. The current northern entrance, Country road 7900 to 7950, directs hikers and campers to the Visitor Center. Today the ruins are all located on the mostly one way Chaco Loop, which can be gated at night to keep the ruins safe from looting and other illegal activities.

At the western end of the box canyon loop you will walk by Casa Chiquita (Spanish for "Small House"), a small minor ruin that's never been excavated: a square block of 34 small rooms built around an elevated kiva. Like nearby Kin Kletso, Chiquita has McElmo style core-and-veneer masonry. A large masonry dam northeast of the Chiquita once blocked at least a portion of the mouth of Cly's Canyon and may have helped collect and channel water into nearby agricultural fields.

I would not spend much time at Casa Chiquita, because there are more interesting sites to explore up ahead. In fact, as you leave Casa Chiquita behind, the once massive Penasco Blanco begins to come into view high on West Mesa. This will be our primary destination on the West Mesa hike.

First, though, about a half mile beyond Casa Chiquita, we come to a side trail that branches off toward North Mesa. The Petroglyph Trail, as it's called, will take you to six panels of petroglyphs carved in the soft sandstone of the cliff. These six panels represent the largest collection of petroglyphs in the canyon, stick figures of animals and humans engaged in a variety of activities, from farming, hunting, dancing, and participating in religious ceremonies. You will see Navajo and Anglo inscriptions as well, carved into the cliff by itinerant visitors to the canyon. You can spend hours reading the inscriptions and deciphering the stories told by the petroglyphs, but I would advise against spending too much time here, as the trail is long and we have come only halfway, with the more difficult, climbing portion of the trail ahead.

About a mile beyond the Petroglyph Trail we come to a crossroad. We have a decision to make. We can cross Chaco Wash and begin the looping climb up West Mesa to Penasco Blanco, or we can swing north on the old Navajo wagon road that will take us around behind West Mesa to the convergence of the Chaco Wash and the wide, sandy Escavada wash that merge to become the Chaco River. My advice would be to visit the convergence first, if you have any interest in seeing the flat bottomland where the Chacoan waterworks were located. This side trip will add another mile or so total to your hike, but if you're like me, you have more energy on

Petroglyph Panel.

Convergence of the Chaco and Escavada washes.

Chaco Wash.

the way in than on the way out. And the convergence is interesting, with a naturally occurring sand dune that may have damned the Chaco Wash in the past, creating a lake. You can walk over terrain where lidar and aerial photography have identified Chacoan dams, canals, and ponds used for irrigation and, apparently, recreation.

Now back to the main trail. First we head south, crossing Chaco Wash, which these days is usually bone dry. The wash is shallow and easy to cross here. Today the wash is dominated by greasewood and saltbush, not the cottonwoods and willows that grew along the banks during Chaco's zenith. Likewise, the greater canyon was long ago denuded of the juniper and pinon trees that Chacoans depended upon for building materials, fires, and shade.

Once on the other side of the wash, you quickly begin the long, gradual climb up the trail to the top of West Mesa. Lots to see here, including ridges topped with red lichen that look like they've been dipped in red chile, fossils of sea creatures who lived eons ago, and boulders as large as houses. Soon you will find yourself approaching an overhang along the cliff. Look up and you will see the most famous pictograph at Chaco: an exploding star believed by some to be a representation of the 1054 Supernova that was visible for over twenty days and present at night for nearly two years. Just below the "Supernova Pictograph," on a vertical ledge, is another pictograph that may be a representation of the 1066 appearance of Haley's Comet. Both of these dramatic cosmic events were clearly visible in the sky over Chaco and may have induced panic in Chacoans who lived by, and believed in, a dependably regular cosmos. In fact, some researchers have speculated that these two cosmic events may have weakened the rule of the altepetl at Chaco by calling into question their ability to understand, predict, and therefore control the heavens.

Don't linger too long at the pictographs, though. You still have a mile climb to the top of West Mesa. The trail loops around to the southeast, then to the west. As you near the top, climbing over the last ridge, you begin to see the jagged walls of Penasco Blanco (Spanish for "White Cliff"). You don't get a sense of how large the ruin is until you get closer and begin walking around the unusual oval-shaped perimeter, which includes a group of rooms and a Great Kiva outside of the crumbling wall.

One of the original Great Houses at Chaco, built around the same time as Pueblo Bonito, Penasco Blanco was once a three-story Great House with 215 rooms and four Great Kivas with mixed masonry styles. It was oriented to the lunar major standstill, according to the Solstice Project. As the westernmost Great House in Chaco perched high on West Mesa, Penasco Blanco commanded the western entrance to the canyon and guarded the Chacoan waterworks below. Looking east from its elevated location you can view almost the entire canyon along an 8-mile axis line to Pueblo Bonito and Una Vida. You might notice the faint traces of an ancient road segment adjacent to the external Great Kiva south of the ruin. The road was one of the main entrances into the canyon from the west, connecting Penasco Blanco with the Chuska Mountains. The ruin was only partially excavated in 1923–1927 by Neil M. Judd and the National Geographic Expedition and since then has been allowed to decay gracefully, without any effort to stabilize or otherwise tamper with the ruin. Because of its deteriorating condition, and maybe its isolation on West Mesa, I've always thought Penasco Blanco had a solemn dignity unmatched by any of the other Great Houses at Chaco.

You will also see an interesting group of rooms outside the wall east of the Great House. The roomblock was built on an earthen platform constructed by the Chacoans, similar to the raised plaza at Chetro Ketl. From the rooms on the elevated platform, the Chacoans would have had a panoramic view of all the canyon's mesas and Great Houses.

Supernova pictograph.

Before leaving, I like to walk to the northwestern edge of the mesa and look out over the landscape, even if I've stopped first at the convergence of the Chaco and Escavada washes. You look out on an enormous vista of distant mountains and massive buttes and the Chaco River to the southwest. But I don't stay too long, because it's a long hike back to the Pueblo del Arroyo parking lot. By the time I get back to my Subaru, it's time to call it a day and head to the campground for extended R & R.

Penasco Blanco.

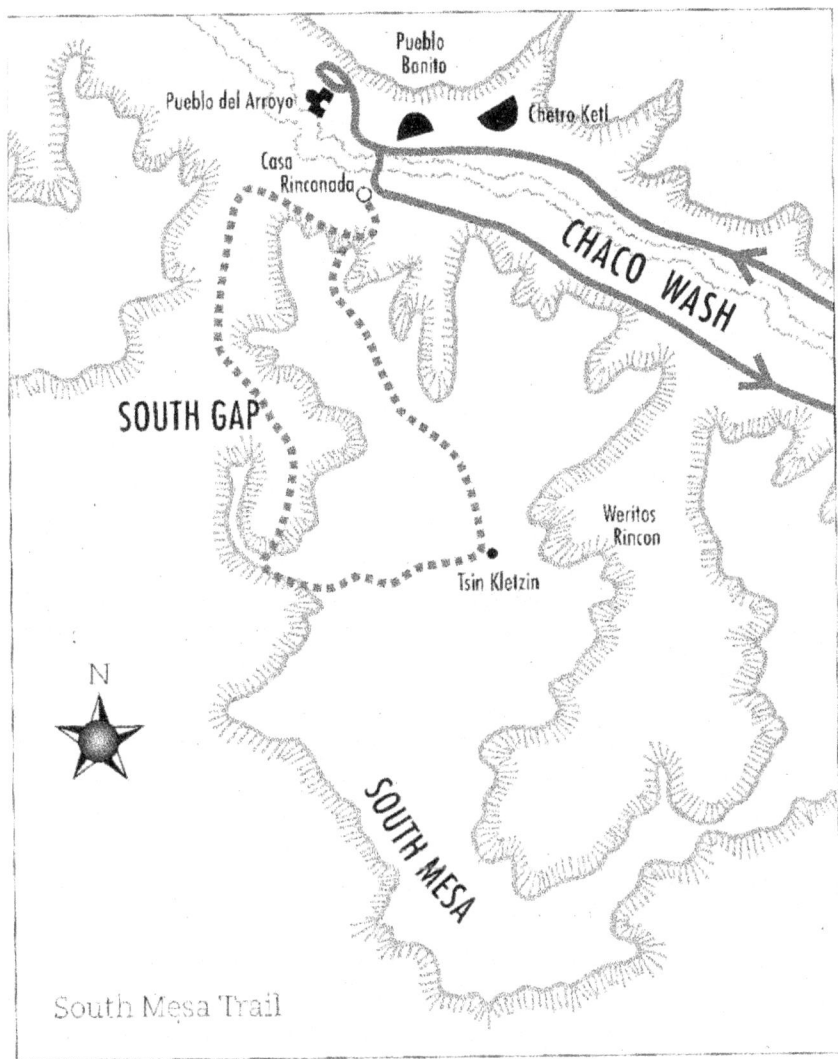

National Park Service Map of South Mesa.

Casa Rinconada.

Trail 4: South Mesa: Casa Rinconada and Tsin Kletsin, South Gap

3.6 miles, 4 hours from the Casa Rinconada parking lot.

For a shorter hike, take the trail from Casa Rinconada to Tsin Kletsin and return by the same route, 2.6 miles, 3 hours.

The trail up South Mesa begins at the Casa Rinconada parking lot. Casa Rinconada is a monster, the largest Great Kiva at Chaco and one of the largest in the entire Southwest, with an average diameter of 63 feet. Remember, Great Kivas were used for ceremonial and religious events. This public function explains some of the intriguing features of Casa Rinconada. For example, if you look carefully you'll see that both the north and south entryways were connected to anterooms that lead into the kiva. The north entry in particular had six rooms attached to its anteroom and then a 39-foot underground passage, 3 feet deep and 3 feet wide, leading into the kiva. You can imagine public ceremonies with dancers, priests, or Kachinas (people dressed as gods) entering the kiva through this passage to perform for the members of the gathered clan.

Inside Casa Rinconada you see the typical features shared by all kivas, including a firebox, masonry vaults, and intermittent niches built into the wall of the kiva. A stone bench for sitting encircles the underground structure, large enough to accommodate dozens of celebrants. Stone stairways lead into the north and south antechambers from which the priests or dancers would emerge. And four large seating pits for roof supports are clearly visible. The supports would have been massive logs cut from forests as far away as fifty miles. The kiva roof would have been constructed with the same materials used for roofs in the Great Houses: wood beams overlaid with willow branches and then layered with mud and juniper bark.

Casa Rinconada was excavated in 1931 by a University of New Mexico/School of American Research field team. The team discovered clusters of roomblocks around Rinconada, primarily to the east and west. Since the units were much simpler in design and construction than the Great Houses on the other side of the canyon, the researchers speculated that the rooms belonged to commoners, workers and laborers who tended the fields, cut and hauled the trees used in the canyon, and built the structures and roads throughout the Chaco.

Leaving Casa Rinconada, the trail leads sharply to the west and then cuts back as you begin to climb South Mesa. It's a long, gradual ascent that takes longer than you think, primarily because the trail is quite steep in some places. Also, the trail is not as clearly marked by cairns as most of the other trails in the canyon, so it's easy to lose track of the route. My guess is that the trail isn't particularly well tended because so few visitors hike up to South Mesa. On any given day during the summer you will find most visitors in Downtown Chaco, but you will also see dozens of hikers climbing atop North Mesa and at least a few on the West Mesa trail. If you chose to climb South Mesa you might find yourself hiking solo.

View from South Mesa.

This is a shame, because South Mesa offers some of the best views of the canyon and its surroundings. The view of the canyon as you climb up South Mesa is spectacular. Pueblo Bonito and Chetro Ketl stand directly across the canyon from the trail. If you're like me, you'll find yourself looking back over your shoulder and stopping repeatedly to take photos. I can only imagine what it must have been like a thousand years ago to descend into this urban center of four—and five-story Great Houses. This view is the closest I'll ever come to understanding that feeling.

Warning: the more times you stop to take photos, the more time you will need to finish the hike. I've learned this the hard way. The South Mesa trail should take no more than three or four hours, but often I will spend an entire afternoon trying to get the perfect angle for a photo of the Great Houses below. Depending on your lens, you can capture Casa Rinconada, Pueblo Bonito, and Chetro Ketl in the same frame. I can spend an hour or so trying to properly align the three structures.

So tear yourself away from the never-ending photo op and forge ahead. You'll climb over an endless succession of ridges until finally, when you're about to give up, you'll come to a narrow trail that cuts through a flat area overgrown with scrub grass, sage, and cactus. There, at the top of the slope, you will see what remains of Tsin Kletsin (Navajo for "Black Wood Place"), a small 70-room Great House. No doubt the ruin will disappoint you at first, having just come from viewing the majestic Pueblo Bonito and Chetro Ketl. But look around. It's the 360-degree views that make this Great House special.

I'll admit, Tsin Kletsin doesn't look like much today. The classic D-shaped Great House with McElmo style masonry veneer has been allowed to deteriorate over the centuries. Its three kivas and two enclosed plazas have never been excavated or stabilized. Because only small amounts of broken pottery have been found near Tsin Kletsin, researchers believe it was used for trading or ceremonial gatherings, not as a residential structure. With a cardinal orientation, Tsin Kletsin is also located on the north-south axis that connects it to Pueblo Bonito in the canyon and Pueblo Alto on North Mesa.

Several Chacoan road fragments have been found near Tsin Kletsin. One leads from Tsin Keltsin north to an ancient stairway down into the canyon. The stairway can be accessed at the pull off just west of the Casa

Tsin Kletsin.

Rinconada Parking Lot. Other road fragments connected Tsin Kletsin to South Gap and the road leading south out of the canyon, all the way to the outlier Kin Ya'a (Navajo for "Tall House") and Hosta Butte.

Here, again, you have a decision to make. If you've paid more attention to your photography than your hiking, as I often do, you can save time by following the trail back down to Casa Rinconada, an easy downhill hike. Or, if you still have the time and energy, you can continue on the trail west to South Gap and then south around the mesa to Rinconada, another two miles. Along the way you can enjoy views of the Chuska Mountains to the west and Shiprock to the northwest. The Chacoans obtained many of the ponderosa pine and fir logs they used in construction from the Chuska Mountains. An estimated 225,000 logs were used at Chaco, some from more than fifty miles away.

South Gap provides a natural break separating South Mesa from West Mesa. At the western edge of South Mesa the man-made trail descends into a box canyon. The cut-out or stairway was built by Navajo sheepherders in the 19th century and provides an easy way to get to the canyon floor. Once you exit the box canyon, you can look for remnants of the ancient Chacoan roads leading into the canyon from the south. The ancient roads stretched

South Gap.

south to outliers and sacred ceremonial places in the landscape like Hosta Butte, thirty miles away.

I have one more attraction to mention here. If you happen to be coming down from South Mesa in late afternoon or early evening, you may be joined by an elk or two. Yes, Chaco has its own elk herd, which numbers about twenty-five, I am told. The sturdy beasts come down from South Mesa to feed on the flora in Chaco Wash and usually don't pay much attention to the puny humans wandering aimlessly, it must seem to them, around the canyon.

Chaco Elk.

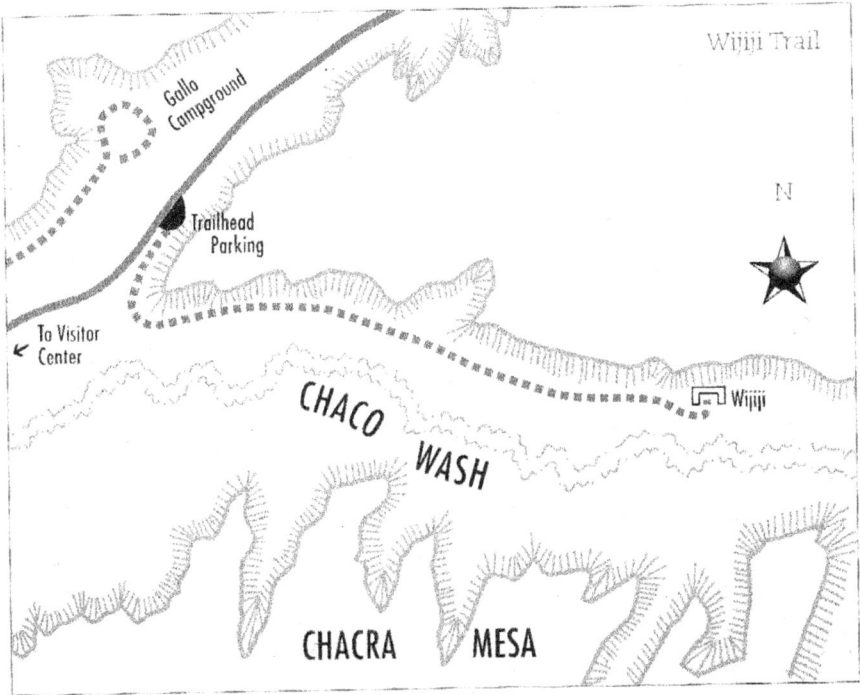

National Park Service Map of Chacra Mesa.

TRAIL 5 / CHACRA MESA: WIJIJI AND CHACRA MESA

3 miles, 3-4 hours, from pull-off along road or Gallo campground.

Unlike the other trails at Chaco, there's no parking lot for the hike east to Wijij (perhaps Navajo for "Black Greasewood"). You can park in the marked pull-off along the Chaco Loop just east of the campground entrance, or if you're camping, you can leave your vehicle at the campground and hike over to the trailhead, an easy walk.

The trail to Wijiji, the easternmost Great House in the Park, runs alongside Chaco Wash and follows Chacra Mesa east. You'll notice how the wash has been affected by extensive arroyo cutting, which has carved out side channels and gullies that divert much needed water from the canyon

Chaco Canyon from the Wijiji trail.

floor. Arroyo cutting can be incredibly destructive to agriculture and could have contributed to the hard times that befell Chaco in the 13th century.

Unlike the more rigorous trails at Chaco, the trail to Wijiji involves no climbing or difficult stretches. It's a flat, leisurely hike that I like to do early in the morning when I'm just getting started. I love to take my time, walking toward the new sun and enjoying the fresh morning air. A fantastic way to wake up! Along the way you can pause for photos of Chacra Mesa to the south or for a panorama shot of the canyon behind you. From the trail you can see how the canyon opens up, with Fajada Butte and South Mesa to the left, and North Mesa to the right. The ruins of Pueblo Bonito and Chetro Ketl are just visible if you look closely. This is the view Chacoans would have had entering the canyon from the east.

Wijiji seems to materialize out of the canyon wall to the north. Like Penasco Blanco and Tsin Kletsin, it commands an entrance to the canyon. With a C-shaped ground-plan and two or three stories, Wijiji had a total of 225 rooms, 100 of them on the ground floor. Wijiji has the reputation of being the most symmetrical of Chacoan Great Houses, with two symmetrically placed kivas in its north room block and identical east and west wings. It has a south-southeast orientation, not quite cardinal and not quite solstitial.

Chacra Mesa.

Wijiji.

There are no Great Kivas in the ruin itself (though there is one about 1/2 mile away) and not much evidence of residential use. For example, no trash midden has been found in the area. The speculation is that Wijiji was used for visitors, either traders or pilgrims arriving for calendrical religious ceremonies at Chaco. Wijiji has not been excavated.

I like to linger at Wijiji, poke around the ruin and the arroyo, take some panoramic shots of the canyon and look for trails leading up to the mesa tops. If you're patient you can find animal trails leading up North Mesa and Chacra Mesa especially, because Navajo sheepherders have a long history of grazing their herds on Chacra long after the Ancestral Puebloans abandoned the canyon. I have yet to see any elk this far east in the canyon, but who knows, maybe next visit.

Before you leave Wijiji, you'll want to visit the pictograph panel about 300 feet east of the ruin. Follow the marked trail to an overhang in the cliff, where you will find two red animal images surrounded by handprints. The red tint is unusual—and very striking.

That's about it for Wijiji. You can explore Chaco Wash or, if you want to go further, hike along Chacra Mesa and enjoy the solitude. You won't find any hikers out here.

Wijiji Detail

Though it's not on the park maps, an important Basketmaker site known as Shabik'eshchee Village is located on the northern escarpment of Chacra Mesa, overlooking Chaco Wash, about a mile east of Wijiji. One of the best known pithouse villages in the entire Four Corners area, Shabik'eshchee includes at least 64 pithouses, 48 storage bins, and possibly a Great Kiva. Tree ring dating has determined that at least part of the village dates from the mid 500s A.D. Some archaeologists believe that a second occupation occurred sometime after 700 A.D., a precursor to the Chaco expansion in the 9th century. They point to the ruins of a proto kiva, a courtyard, and a few pithouses built later than the early settlement. Today, nothing much remains to identify the site, just a scattering of earthen mounds and partially filled pits. Still, it's a humble experience to stand there where 1500 years ago the ancestors of the Ancestral Puebloans created the beginnings of the Chaco phenomenon.

If you were to follow Chaco Wash for another 12 miles you would come to Pueblo Pintado, a Chacoan outlier outside the canyon proper. We'll visit Pintado in the Chaco Outlier section below.

You can easily hike to Wijiji in the morning and then go for one of the longer, more rigorous hikes in the afternoon. That, to me, makes for a perfect day at Chaco.

Fajada Butte.

Roadside Ruins / Una Vida and Hungo Pavi

Una Vida

The final two ruins in the canyon, Una Vida and Hungo Pavi, require no hiking. The short, accessible trail to Una Vida (Spanish for "One Life") begins at the Visitor Center parking lot and takes you west a couple of hundred yards to the ruin, an irregular D-shaped Great House snuggled against North Mesa. The construction of Una Vida began around 860, which makes it one of the three oldest Great Houses in the Canyon, with Pueblo

Una Vida, National Park Service photo.

Bonito and Penasco Blanco. My guess is that the early Chacoans liked this site because Una Vida overlooks the Fajada Gap area and the convergence of the Chaco and Fajada washes, and there is widespread evidence of water diversion and irrigation. In a canyon as dry as Chaco, access to water would have been a determining factor when it came to building location.

By the time construction ended about 1095, the Great House had 160 rooms, most of them in the two-story northern and western room blocks. You will also find four kivas and one Great Kiva. The ruin has a southeast orientation, possibly aligned to the lunar major standstill, according to the Solstice Project. Una Vida was partially excavated by Gordon Vivian and the National Park Service in the late 1950s. In 1987 it was cleared and mapped by the National Park Service Chaco Project led by Nancy J. Akins and William B. Gillespie.

Just up the slope to the west of Una Vida you will find a wall of petroglyphs that are some of the finest in Chaco Canyon. There are human and animal figures, geometric designs, and astronomical and migration symbols. I could spend hours here reading the symbols and trying to

Hungo Pavi with ancient stairway to the left and Mockingbird Canyon to the right, National Park Service photo.

decipher the stories they tell, some of them as much as 1,300 years old. But I never seem to have enough time, there's so much to see and do at Chaco.

What I like about Una Vida, in addition to its spectacular wall of rock art, is its proximity to the Visitor Center. At the Visitor Center you can tour the small museum and browse the gift shop, then step outside for a short walk along North Mesa. Also, the parking lot and vicinity is a terrific place for sunset and night photography. You have an open view of the canyon, especially Fajada Gap and Fajada Butte. The ruins are closed at sunset, but I've found it possible to walk part-way down the trail to Una Vida to snap night photos. On a clear night the sky above Chaco Canyon is alive with millions of stars, the white milky way running through the sky like a river. On nights like these it's difficult to call it a day and return to camp.

HUNGO PAVI

If you're driving, the small ruin of Hungo Pavi is the first stop on the 8-mile loop through Chaco Canyon. It's halfway between Una Vida and Pueblo Bonito, about two miles west of the Visitor Center. Its location at the mouth of the Mockingbird Canyon makes Hungo Pavi special, because Mockingbird is a sweet little canyon perfect for a short hike, a meditation, or a photo shoot. Visually striking, the canyon provides spectacular views of the canyon walls, the light always changing as the sun moves from east to west.

You can access the Hungo Pavi trail at the parking area along Chaco Loop near the ruin, a quarter mile hike up the ridge. The trail takes you first to the top of the western room block from where you look down on the beehive rooms and kivas of the D-shaped Great House. At its zenith Hungo Pavi had as many as 140 rooms. Follow the trail into the plaza, past the Great Kiva, and then over the eastern room block to the massive rear wall running parallel to the mesa. If you stop at the northeast corner of the ruin and look carefully at the cliff wall, you will see ancient steps carved out of the rock. The stairway allowed Chacoans to climb to the top of North Mesa and, presumably, access the ancient road grid that radiated out from Pueblo Alto in all directions. From there you can wander into Mockingbird Canyon or follow the trail west around the ruin and back to the parking area.

The construction of Hungo Pavi occurred in two major stages. The north room block, backed up against the mesa, began in the late 900s or early 1000s. The eastern and western room blocks were added in the mid 11th century. In its final form the Great House had as many as three stories with a single-story wall around its enclosed plaza. Today you see two kivas, an elevated kiva in the north room block and the Great Kiva in the plaza.

Hungo Pavi has a Cardinal or north-south orientation slightly tipped toward the southeast, possibly an equinox alignment, according to the Solstice Project. It has never been excavated.

Author's camp at Gallo.

Gallo Campground and Facilities

If you're planning to camp at Chaco, here are a few things you should know about the campground. Gallo Campground is small with only 32 individual campsites, and is generally booked solid from May through October. Reservations are required and can be made at the Recreation.gov website. The fee at the time this book was published is $20 per night, $10 per night for seniors with Senior or Access cards. Campers should check in with the park ranger at the entrance to Gallo before proceeding. Arrival time is noon, and departing campers must be out by 11 a.m. the next day. Maximum length of stay is fourteen days.

Two group campsites are available, each accommodating up to thirty people and five vehicles. Group stays are limited to seven days. The group rate is $60 per might. Group sites are designed for tent camping and can't accommodate RVs. One campsite, 16, is designated as handicapped accessible, although I think most of the tent sites are equally accessible, as are the restroom facilities. You can check photos of the sites online at the Recreation.gov website to get a view of each site's layout.

Each campsite has a picnic table, fire grate, and tent pad made of sand. Restroom facilities are generally good, with running water and sinks for basic hygiene. All campsites come with parking spaces for one or two vehicles adjoining the site, which makes setting up camp fast and easy.

What I love about the campground is the quiet. Maybe it's my imagination, but Chaco campers tend to be of the reflective sort anyway, not the wild party animals you find at some other more easily accessible campgrounds. Only once in all my stays at Gallo have I encountered a loud, rambunctious group of teenagers with little parental control. You can pretty much count on a quiet evening and a good night's sleep.

You will find two extra features that make Gallo even more interesting. First, a small but real Chacoan ruin can be found against the mesa wall between sites 25 and 26. Not much to look at when compared to the enormous ruins in the canyon proper, but it gives you a hint of what lies ahead. Small ruins like this are ubiquitous in and around the canyon. Over

Fajada Butte at sunset.

2,000 such ruins, most of them small, have been identified in the greater Chaco area.

The other feature, which I particularly appreciate, is the Chaco Canyon Overlook Trail that begins at the sign in the campground. It takes you on a gradual hike up to the top of North Mesa to a point where you can see a large portion of the canyon. The view of Fajada Butte is especially striking. Halfway up the trail you will see a cave, usually off limits, used by Zuni, Acoma, and other Puebloans for occasional ceremonies. These Puebloans consider Chaco their ancestral homeland.

The Overlook Trail is perfect for a quick hike late in the afternoon when you don't want to drive back down the 8-mile Chaco Loop but still want to do a little hiking. Toward the end of the day I always appreciate not having to drive. Since the trail is only about 1.5 miles to the overlook, you can do it fairly quickly and then get back to camp to enjoy a cold beverage.

I've also found the overlook a perfect place for sunrise/sunset photography. From the overlook you get a clear view of both the eastern and western horizons, much clearer than down in the canyon. Just make sure to bring a flashlight or headlamp if you go up to catch the sunset, just in case you stay on top a little longer than you intended and have to make your way back in the dark.

Back in the mid 1970s, when Gallo had few of the amenities it now has, I remember a nearly deserted campground, with only a couple of tents and a stray VW van for company. Back then few people visited Chaco, and even fewer stayed to camp in what then resembled a hot parking lot. Occasionally one of the rangers would wander into the campground to make small talk with the campers. And I remember one night in particular. We were sitting around a campfire, listening to a ranger tell Chaco ghost stories. Sometimes during the night they heard noises and saw lights moving through the ruins, she said. Noises, lights, and a cold feeling that comes over your skin when you are in the presence of … what?

She ended our conversation by saying that everyone assumed Chaco was a holy place of peace and light, but if you lived here for any length of time you began to have a different view, a darker view. Bad things had happened here, and you could still feel the bad vibes, she said. She never used the word evil, just bad.

On the rest of that visit and the next couple of times I camped at Chaco I always felt a sense of unease, not of foreboding exactly, but of vulnerability. I mean, there was hardly anyone else in the canyon back in those days, so it was like finding yourself alone in a spooky ruin. Something like that. But all that changed as the years passed and I encountered more and more people at Chaco. Nothing like a crowd to drive away the spirits, I guess. So Chaco has a different feeling today. Safer, to be sure, but not quite as connected to the presence of its ancestors.

Sometimes, though, when you find yourself alone in the quiet of Penasco Blanco or another of the more distant Great Houses, you start to get that physical sensation or intimation that tells you the ancestors are present.

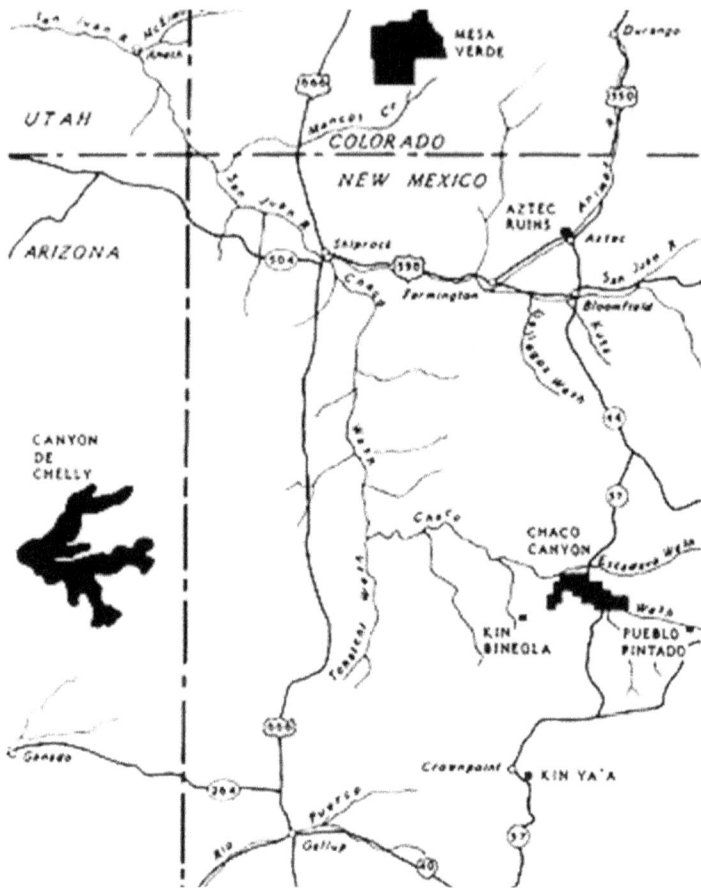

Chaco Outliers.

CHACO OUTLIERS

Outliers were Great Houses in the larger Chaco network. They were connected to Chaco Canyon, the Center Place, by ancient roads and by a line-of-sight communication system of fire towers. Scattered throughout the Four Corners area, they shared the same language, culture, and architecture (Great Kivas, enclosed plazas, etc.). They served as satellite outposts, providing security but also bringing nearby communities into Chaco for religious ceremonies and trade fairs. Outliers also provided food and other resources for the Great Houses in the canyon. Some, like Kin Klizhin, maintained large agricultural fields to supply the Center Place.

Kin Klizhin

Technically, Kin Klizhin may not be considered an outlier since it's located at the southwestern edge of Chaco Culture Historical Park, but it takes a great deal of effort and patience to get to the small ruin. You have to take NM Route 57 south of the Visitor Center, turn right on an unmarked dirt road, and drive a total of 12 miles over very rough terrain to reach Kin Klizhin. I repeat, you should only attempt to navigate this road in a rugged 4-wheel drive vehicle.

The ruin barely qualifies as a Great House, having only sixteen rooms, eight of them on the ground floor in a single room block running north and south. However, there are three kivas, two Great Kivas and one tower kiva that was once three or four stories high and apparently used as an observation and signaling station. The tower can be seen from Tsin Kletsin on the South Mesa. An irregular D-shaped ruin, the Great House was tipped slightly to face the southeast. Tree ring dates collected by Florence Hawley in 1932 dated Kin Klizhin about 1087, but the ruin was never excavated.

For me, the isolation of the ruin is its main attraction. The ruin itself

Kin Klizhin, National Park Service photo.

won't take you more than a few minutes to inspect, but the landscape surrounding Kin Klizhin is enchanting. You can spend a considerable amount of time here just hiking around Kin Klizhin Wash east of the ruin where the inhabitants tended valley fields irrigated by an elaborate water system that included a masonry and mud dam, as well as a canal and ditch system.

You might also be able to make out the ancient road from South Gap that passes by Kin Klizhin on its way south to Kin Bineola, a much larger and more interesting outlier about six miles southwest of Kin Klizhin. An E-shaped Great House with 200 rooms and 11 kivas, the oldest part of Kin Bineola has been dated to between 940–945, which makes it one of the earliest Great Houses in the Chaco area, almost as old as Pueblo Bonito, Penasco Blanco and Una Vida. Like Kin Klizhin, Kin Bineola's location allowed it to take advantage of the farming potential of the valley. Water control systems along Kin Bineola Wash made large scale agriculture possible.

Unfortunately for hikers, Kin Bineola is not open to the public.

Pueblo Pintado.

Pueblo Pintado detail.

Pueblo Pintado

As the easternmost Great House in the immediate Chaco area, Pueblo Pintado stands high on a ridge overlooking the small Navajo community of the same name. Pintado has been on Navajo land for centuries. It was the first Chacoan site encountered in 1849 by the initial U.S. military reconnaissance expedition into Navajo country. A Spanish guide called the ruin Pueblo Pintado, Spanish for "Painted Town."

Even though the ruin is only sixteen miles southeast of Pueblo Bonito as the crow flies, the most direct route by car is to exit the canyon on Country Road 7950 and proceed to where it intersects Country Road 7900. Instead of turning left to return to Highway 550, take a right and continue heading southeast and then southwest on 7900. You will see the ruin on the right as you come into the Navajo community. Believe me, this is by far the easiest way to get to Pueblo Pintado.

The irregular D-shaped Great House has never been excavated or even stabilized, as far as I can tell. The ruin has a southeast orientation, possibly aligned to the minor lunar standstill, according to the Solstice Project. Constructed in the 1060s, Pueblo Pintado commanded the eastern approach to Chaco Canyon. The 135 rooms include ninety on the ground floor, forty on a second floor, and five on a third floor. There's also evidence of nineteen kivas among the ruins, as well as one Great Kiva southeast of the ruin. Not much of the original Great House remains today. You will find fragments of walls and indentations where underground rooms and kivas once existed. Even so, it's an interesting place to explore. You can enjoy a spectacular view from the ridge, overlooking Chaco Wash and the Navajo community below. As you hike around the area you will see additional ruins on the ridge. Indeed, some thirty small ruins have been discovered around the Great House.

Salmon Ruins (Courtesy of *Rational Observer*)

To me, Pueblo Pintado always seems more of a stopping point for travelers on their way to Chaco for trade or religious ceremonies than an agricultural community. It may also have served a defensive purpose as well, because it does protect the entrance to Chaco proper. Two ancient road segments can be distinguished, one extending southwest from the ruin about two miles. The other segment extends north from the ruin about two miles, where it enters Chaco Wash by means of a stairway carved into the sandstone cliff. As I mentioned, you could hike west along Chaco Wash all the way back to Gallo Campground, about 12 miles.

I don't have time for that, but I do enjoy poking around the ruins and the outbuildings, doing a little free-style hiking without any particular destination, just to see what I can find. One of the sad things about Pueblo Pintado is that it's totally isolated without any supervision by the National Park Service. As a result looters have severely vandalized the ruin, leaving dozens of pits and mounds of dirt behind from their digging. It's a shame, but the National Park Service just doesn't have the resources to police a ruin this remote.

Salmon Ruins

Imagine you were able to hike the Great North Road from Pueblo Alto north to Salmon Ruins. Along the way you would encounter a series of smaller Great Houses: Pierre's Site, Halfway House, and Twin Angels.

Though small, averaging fifteen to twenty rooms, the sites served important functions as signaling stations and way stations for Chacoans traveling north to the larger Great Houses at Salmon Ruins and Aztec Ruins, located in Bloomington and Aztec, New Mexico, respectively.

Since few people attempt to walk the entire Great North Road today, for many obvious reasons, I would recommend option number two: driving. You can get from Chaco Canyon to Salmon Ruins easily by continuing north on U.S. Highway 550 for about forty miles to Bloomfield, where you turn west on U.S. Highway 64. Salmon is a few miles down the road on the left side of the highway. You can't miss the Visitor Center and Museum.

Salmon Ruins may have been the original terminus of the Great North Road, before Aztec replaced it a generation later. Salmon was built in the 1080s and 1090s at the height of Chaco's culture, which at the time was expanding and colonizing the Four Corners area. When its location on the north bank of the San Juan River proved less than ideal because of flooding and other problems, the Chacoans moved a few miles north to Aztec, a more stable location on the Animas River.

Located forty-five miles north of Pueblo Bonito, Salmon was a three-story rectangular Great House that originally contained 275-325 rooms, with a tower kiva and a Great Kiva south of the ruin. Its configuration was almost identical to Hungo Pavi with a Cardinal or north-south orientation, possibly aligned to the equinox. Formerly owned by the Salmon family, the property is currently owned by the San Juan County Museum Association, which has maintained the site and the accompanying museum since 1969.

The short trail through the ruin begins at the Visitors Center, near the old Salmon homestead. You begin by walking along the 400-foot-long north wall, which has been stabilized by adding mounds of dirt. You will notice portions of a third-story interior wall, where you can look down into what was once a round tower kiva. A "Lizard Woman" mural was found in the kiva and is on display in the adjoining Museum. The trail takes you around the Great House to the open plaza area. Here you can view the ruin's only Great Kiva, which has a 58 ft. diameter, and then head back to the Visitor Center and Museum. It's not much of a hike, just over a half mile, and the ruin itself is not terribly exciting, especially after Chaco Canyon. So if serious hiking—or camping—is what you're looking for, you may want to skip Salmon Ruins.

If you do stop, the Salmon Museum is definitely worth investigating.

Aztec West.

The ruin was only was excavated in the 1970s by Cynthia Irwin-Williams of Eastern New Mexico University, in conjunction with the San Juan County Museum. An estimated 1.5 million artifacts were recovered during the excavation, a good many of them on display in the Museum. Interestingly, the great number and kind of artifacts uncovered at Salmon Ruins suggest a residential usage, rather than a ceremonial or commercial usage. This function distinguishes Salmon from the Great Houses at Chaco, which primarily served ceremonial and commercial functions.

AZTEC RUINS

Aztec is an easy drive from Salmon Ruins. Continue west on U.S. Highway 64 for about five miles, turn right and head north on State Road 516 to the city of Aztec, about fifteen miles. Turn left on Ruins Road and follow the signs through a residential neighborhood to Aztec Ruins National Monument, which like Chaco is an UNESCO World Heritage Site (since 1987).

When the Chacoans abandoned Salmon Ruins about 1125, they moved north along the Chaco Meridian to Aztec, which became the new

Inside Aztec's restored kiva.

Interior rooms, Aztec West.

terminus of the Great North Road. Aztec is due north of Pueblo Alto, Pueblo Bonito (sort of), and Tsin Kletsin. By the early 1200s the Chacoans were abandoning Aztec, moving back and forth to the Mesa Verde area. The entire Aztec occupation lasted from about 1110 to 1275.

Some researchers have speculated that Aztec was intended to be the new Chaco, with as many as six Great Houses and dozens of smaller sites spread out over 1.5 miles near the Animas River. Archaeologists have discovered shrines, mounds, stone quarries, earthen platforms, and ancient road fragments scattered over what's called the Aztec Bench. Of the six Great Houses only West Ruin has been excavated. East Ruin and Earl Morris Ruin appear to be as massive as West Ruin, which in its heyday was a three-story Great House of 500 rooms built on a rectangular or irregular D-shaped ground plan. Like the early Pueblo Bonito before its north-south realignment, West Ruin has a southeastern or solstitial alignment.

The half-mile, paved trail starts at the Visitor Center and is wheelchair accessible. The trail takes you into the main plaza area to Aztec's main attraction: a completely restored Great Kiva. The kiva was excavated in 1921 by archaeologist Earl Morris, who finished rebuilding the structure in 1934. The minute you step inside you feel as though you've entered a new dimension of time and space. The dim lights along the stairway draw you down to the bottom of the kiva and trigger your imagination, taking you to a different world, the world of the Ancestral Puebloans before the arrival of Europeans on their continent. You see the fire pit and the niches and benches along the wall, where 900 years ago the people of Aztec met for social and religious ceremonies and celestial celebrations. It's a unique, extraordinary place that Chaco enthusiasts will never forget. I typically spend more time in the restored Great Kiva than I do in the rest of West Ruin. I should add that the lighting in the kiva is perfect for indoor photography. The photos I've taken inside the kiva are some of my best.

When you step back outside, you will notice a row of small rooms, fifteen of them, that ring the outside of the kiva. What these rooms were used for is not fully understood. As you continue on the trail you will come to another Great Kiva, with a domed or cribbed roof composed of timbers layered and angled in a basket weaving effect. If you look up at the second story wall fragment on your right, you will notice a corner doorway connecting two rooms. Corner doorways and windows like these, similar to what we saw at Pueblo Bonito, are unique to Chacoan Great Houses. Notice, also, the T-shaped doors that open onto the plaza area, another feature unique to Chaco-style architecture.

At the northwest corner of the Great House you will enter a series of rooms that may remind you of the interior of Pueblo Bonito. The rooms are dark and the doorways are low, making for tricky walking, so watch your step. When you come to the last row of rooms inside the rear wall of the Great House you will see a doorway partially closed off by an 800-year-old mat of willows sewn with yucca cord made by the original inhabitants of the ruin. The doorways along the south wall of these rooms blocked off by glass were the original entrances.

Once outside, the trail takes you behind the Great House to yet another Great Kiva, where you will discover another of Aztec's unique features: tri-walls. Tri-walled structures are rare in the Southwest. Only one tri-wall has been found among all the Great Houses in Chaco (at Pueblo de Arroyo). By contrast, there are as many as seven tri-walled structures in West Ruin, possibly more. The cultural or symbolic significance of tri-walls is unknown. On the way back to the Visitor Center you're presented with a view of the entire length of the north wall, still more or less plumb after 800-900 years.

Excavations at Aztec started in 1916, conducted by Earl Morris for the American Museum of Natural History in New York. Morris worked at Aztec for seven seasons excavating and stabilizing West Ruin. In the early 1930s he reconstructed the Great Kiva.

In recent years the National Park Service has offered irregular guided tours of the unexcavated ruins at Aztec. You can sign up for the next tour, whenever it's offered, at the Visitor Center. One caution, though: if they notify you by phone or email, you have to be ready to go on a day's notice.

Like Salmon Ruins, Aztec doesn't offer much of an opportunity to hike. Or camp. For that we have to go to our last two outliers: Chimney Rock and Canyon de Chelly.

CHIMNEY ROCK

Chimney Rock Pueblo is the highest, most northeastern, and most dramatic of all Chaco outliers. Located high on a mesa top seventeen miles west of Pagosa Springs in southern Colorado, it overlooks the San Juan Mountains and the Piedra River. It's about a seventy-five mile drive from

Chimney Rock's Great House.

Aztec Ruins. You take New Mexico 550 north from Aztec to State Road 160 just south of Durango, Colorado. Turn right and head east on Highway 160 to State Road 151 south. The turn–off to Chimney Rock will be three miles south on the right side of the highway.

The 4,000-acre Chimney Rock National Monument includes eight villages spread out over eight mesas. The two trails open to the public are both located on the same mesa. The Great Kiva Trail is self-guided, but the more dangerous Great Pueblo Trail, which takes you from an elevation of 7,200 feet to 7,600 feet, must be guided. Tours leave from the Visitor Center (or Cabin as it's called here) between 10:30 a.m. and 3 p.m. daily. The monument stays open from May 15 to September 30, then closes for the winter months when heavy snow makes the roads and trails impassable.

No latecomer in the declining days of the Pax Chaco, Chimney Rock dates from as early as 950. The Great House itself has been dated from the 1070s or 1080s, when the Chaco culture was at its zenith. In fact, the masonry of the Chimney Rock Pueblo is the sophisticated types 3 and 4 core-and-veneer construction of Pueblo Bonito and Chetro Ketl. It's as if the Chaco masons, once they finished with Downtown Chaco, caught the first caravan headed up the Great North Road for southern Colorado. Equally intriguing, the Chimney Rockers began a mass abandonment around 1125,

The chimneys of Chimney Rock.

the same time as the Ancestral Puebloans to the south began to abandon Chaco. All of them migrated west and south.

I'm not a big fan of guided tours, especially when I'm hiking, but I can understand the reasons for making the Great Pueblo Trail guided. The tour gathers at the Visitor Center next to the parking lot and then proceeds up a narrow escarpment with spectacular 360-degree views. It would be easy to get carried away by the views and miss a step, which could result in a nasty fall. I always tag along at the end of the group, half listening to the tour guide while I take notes and photographs. The trail is only two-thirds of a mile round trip, but it rises steeply over rough terrain, so you should be in reasonably good shape.

Toward the top you first encounter a structure called the "Guard House," a round tower that may have been designed for the line-of-sight communication system used by the Chacoans. Fires from the tower could be seen on Huerfano Butte, some 45 miles to the south, and from there relayed to Pueblo Alto in Chaco Canyon. A short distance beyond the Guard House you will approach the Great House, originally a two-story structure with 35 ground floor rooms, 20 second story rooms, and two kivas. As the tour guide will explain, it's an L-shaped ruin oriented to the northeast and perfectly aligned to see the moon rise between the two rock chimneys on the edge of the causeway near winter solstice. Even more of a spectacle occurs every 18.6 years when the rising moon seems to hover in place between the chimneys during a major northern standstill. All this has been documented and recreated by researchers including teams led by J. McKim Malville, the author of *Guide to Prehistoric Astronomy in the Southwest*. I highly recommend his work.

The tour up the escarpment to the Great House takes about an hour, but it always seems shorter to me, never giving me enough time to both look around and finish my photography. So be sure to make good use of your time, whatever your preferences. You won't be able to get dangerously close to the chimneys, for obvious reasons; they are, after all, perched at the edge of a precipice. Even so, the 360-degree view of the San Juan Mountains is nothing short of breathtaking.

Back at the Visitor Center you can take a break and then head downhill on the Great Kiva Tour, which is about the same distance round-trip as the Pueblo Tour. This one you can do on your own and take as much time as you want. If you follow the signs, your first stop will be the Great Kiva constructed about 1084. With a diameter of 44 feet, this is the largest kiva at Chimney Rock. One unusual feature you will notice is that it has no roof support pits, leading archaeologists who have excavated here to question whether the kiva ever had a roof. If not, it certainly would not have been used during the winter months, which can be brutal in the Pagosa Springs/Wolf Creek area, with several feet of snow.

Just north of the Great Kiva you come to a pithouse dating from 1078. The open format allows you to see the various features of pithouse construction, from the sandstone walls to the roof made of sticks and mud. Four wooden posts supported the roof, which had a ladder entrance through the center of the roof. A ventilation shaft on the south side of the building allowed for air, with a" deflector" stone to distribute the air around the pit house and funnel smoke from the fire pit up through the ladder hole in the top of the roof. If you've ever spent time in a teepee or yurt, you'll be familiar with the heating and ventilation system.

As you walk along the trail you will notice mounds of unexcavated pithouses and midden mounds where broken pottery, animal bones, and other bits of trash were tossed. You will also pass ancient fields, where irrigation ditches and dams similar to those in Chaco were used. Take your time here to admire the view of the Piedra River below and the finger-shaped mesas and ridges surrounding the river. On one of these ridges, the so-called Peterson Ridge, a village of thirty unexcavated pithouses and a C-shaped Chacoan Great House overlook the river.

Chimney Rock became a national monument in 2012. It's located on land managed by the San Juan National Forest. It was excavated first by J. A. Jeancon of the Colorado Historical Society in the 1920s and more recently by Frank Eddy in 1970, and by Brenda K. Todd and Stephen H. Lekson in 2009.

You won't find a campground at Chimney Rock, but you can do both the pueblo and kiva trails in a morning or an afternoon and then be on your way to the San Juan Mountains to find a longer hiking trail and a campground. Or you can head southwest toward Canyon de Chelly, our final Chaco outlier.

Canyon de Chelly

Let me confess that Canyon de Chelly is my favorite of all the Chaco outliers because of its long hike down into the canyon on the White House Trail. The easiest way to get to Canyon de Chelly is to take I-40 west from Albuquerque to Gallup, take Highway 491 north to State Road 264 west into Arizona. At Burnside, just past Ganado, turn north on Highway 191, which will take you to Chinle , three miles from the mouth of the canyon. When I was younger I would take a series of zig-zag back roads from Chaco to Chinle, but those days are long gone. I take more direct routes today, now that time doesn't seem nearly as expansive as it did back in the 1970s when I first started hiking these trails.

Canyon de Chelly is one of the oldest continuously occupied sites in North America. Archaeological evidence suggests humans have occupied the area for about 5,000 years. A national monument since 1931, the 84,000-acre park is within the Navajo Reservation but administered by the National Park Service. Historically, the canyons included in the monument have been home to a series of overlapping cultures: Archaic from before 1500 B.C. to 200 A.D., Basketmaker from 200 to 750 A.D, Pueblo from 750 to 1300 A.D., Hopi from 1300 to 1600 A.D., and Navajo from 1700 to the present. Archaeologists have identified some 2,500 archaeological sites in and around the canyon.

On the White House Trail.

One particularly infamous episode in the canyon's long history occurred in 1863 during the Indian Wars, when Kit Carson led a military expedition against the Navajo. In the winter of 1864 Carson and his U.S. troops attacked the eastern end of the canyon, driving the Navajo farmers and sheepherders toward the canyon's mouth. Many Navajo were killed in their futile resistance. Carson and his troops destroyed the hogans and orchards of the Navajo and killed their sheep. The Navajo who survived were forced to march over 300 miles to Fort Sumner in what was then New Mexico Territory. Many died along the way. At Fort Sumner poor food, inadequate shelter, and disease further decimated the tribe. Only in 1868 did the U.S. government allow the Navajo to return to their homeland in the canyon.

Back in the 1970s, when I first started camping at Canyon de Chelly, hiking was more or less unrestricted in the canyon. I remember hiking down trails on both the north and south rims, as well as exploring some of the lower trails at the mouth of the canyon, near the campground. Today, the only self-guided trail sometimes available to hikers is the White House Trail on the South Rim of the canyon. Fortunately, this is the most spectacular trail at Canyon de Chelly. The trail begins at the White House Overlook about four miles from the Visitor Center. Ask permission, if posted.

The trail down used to be quite rough, with rocky ledges and boulders

On the canyon floor.

that made walking difficult, but over the years work crews have smoothed the rough terrain and even added concrete in places. But the trail is still steep, which means it's hard on the knees going down and (at an elevation of nearly 6,000 feet) tiring coming back up. What makes the trail so special is that all the way down you're looking at an incredibly beautiful landscape that seems to unfold as you descend into the canyon. Every step of the way presents another photo op for the incredible scenery that surrounds you: the canyon walls, the rock spires and outcroppings, the green fields and orchards along Chinle Wash on the canyon floor. I find myself stopping for photos every few feet on the 600-foot descent, which can irritate the other hikers I'm with. My bad.

On a solo excursion to the canyon back in 1990 I was climbing up the trail, returning to my car, when I heard rocks flying and what sounded like hooves clattering on the rocky trail. I had the good sense to move off to the side, retreating into a narrow enclave, just before a horse burst into sight around a bend below. What I saw startled me: a young Navajo boy was riding a brown and white spotted horse bareback up the trail. Not walking, but riding the horse at a pretty good clip. I was so taken aback that I didn't have the presence of mind to focus my camera and snap a photo of what was

White House Ruin.

a beautiful, if unsettling sight. I worried the boy and his horse were about to plunge off the trail and fall into the canyon. In fact, I was terrified. But by the time I made it to the top, the two of them were long gone.

Park Service literature lists the trail as 2.5 miles round trip, but it seems much longer to me. Not only do I stop for photographs, but I like to meander around on the canyon floor, taking side trips into box canyons or inspecting interesting rock formations on the way to White House Ruin. The trail comes down near Chinle Wash, which in the spring is fed by runoff from the Chuska Mountains east of the canyon. In the spring or after a heavy rain, Chinle Wash can be tricky to cross, which you have to do in order to stay on the White House Trail.

Once you've crossed over Chinle Wash to its north bank, you follow the stream west as it loops around to the right. About halfway to the ruin, you begin you see glimpses of the White House. In recent years trees have grown in front of the lower ruin and partially blocked the view until you get closer. In the hot summer sun, the ruin can appear a bleached white color,

Spider Rock.

but the white in White House comes from the white plaster used to coat the rear wall of the upper ruin, the cliff dwelling. The first thing you notice is the sheer 600-foot cliff, streaked white and black, towering above the ruin. Just the grandeur, the sheer magnificence of the cliff overwhelms. It's the sort of place that makes a person feel humble, very small. I can spend hours here taking photos or just enjoying the strong vibes. It's truly a sacred place.

There's a rise across the wash that provides a platform to sit and meditate. I spent hours here on one visit watching and trying to photograph a pair of golden eagles defending their nest near the top of the cliff from a swooping pack of ravens. For close-up photographs you can walk around the ruin unobstructed, searching for the perfect angle, but you can't enter the rooms or climb on the walls, which are fragile. Usually you will find several Navajo artists selling their pottery or jewelry at tables erected near the front of the ruin. The prices are usually a bargain.

The White House Ruin was constructed and occupied from about 1060 to 1275.

The lower ruin has sixty rooms, while the upper cliff dwelling has only twenty. The masonry is basically the same core-and-veneer construction we saw at Chaco. Similar to Chaco, the Ancestral Puebloans vacated the canyon about 1300, leaving behind some 600 sites, most of them small.

There are several other overlooks on the South Rim, including Junction Overlook, where Canyon del Muerto meets Canyon de Chelly; Tsegi Overlook, above ancient farmlands; Sliding House Overlook, looking down on a ruin by the same name; and Spider Rock Overlook, which looks out on an 800-foot tall sandstone spire. The entire South Rim Drive is 37 miles round trip. On the North Rim you will find three overlooks: Antelope House Overlook, Mummy Cave Overlook, and Massacre Cave Overlook. The North Rim drive is 34 miles round trip.

Except for White House, most of the major ruins in the canyons are on the North Rim and can be visited only when accompanied by Navajo tour guides. You have to check at the Visitor Center for tour times and costs. Antelope Cave, the first overlook on the North Rim Drive, is a mid-size ruin with kivas and a two or three-story tower and an unusual round plaza at the base of a 600-foot cliff. Its name comes from the illustrations of antelope, thought to be the work of Navajo artist Dibe Yazhi, who lived there in the early 1800s.

The next overlook is Mummy Cave, a large ruin of eighty rooms set back in an alcove in the cliff. It's an intimidating, fort-like ruin with a three-story tower erected on a sheer ledge of rock, very similar to the ruins you find at Mesa Verde and other cliff-dwelling sites. It gets its name from the mummified bodies discovered by Archaeologist Earl H. Morris, who excavated multiple ruins in Canyon from 1923–1929. Morris, who was

White House Ruin in B/W.

sponsored primarily by the American Museum of Natural History in New York, returned again in 1932. He had previously excavated at Aztec Ruin, as you will remember.

Massacre Cave, the final overlook on the North Rim Trail, is a small ruin built in another alcove in the cliff. It takes its name from an 1805 massacre in which a Spanish military expedition led by Antonio Narbona killed over a hundred Navajo who had taken shelter there. From here the North Rim continues on as Arizona Highway 64, which will take you back to Highway 191, where you can head north into Utah or back around to the Monument Valley and Kayenta areas, if you wish to continue visiting more sites on the trail of the Ancestral Puebloans.

If you decide to stay for more than one day, Canyon de Chelly does have a campground (and you will find a Holiday Inn and other motels in Chinle). More on that later. First, let me remind you to bring lots of water on your hike down to the White House Ruin. Canyon de Chelly can be brutally hot in the summer, so travel with a good supply of water and wear sun clothing. You don't have to worry about amenities the way you do at Chaco, because you will find gas stations, restaurants, and other amenities you might need in Chinle.

Now to the Cottonwood Campground, run by the Navajo Parks and Recreation Department. The ninety campsites include two group tent sites located in a grove of cottonwood trees, as the name would indicate. The campground can accommodate RVs up to 40 feet in length, but there are no RV hookups. Cottonwood is open all year round on a first come, first serve basis. Each campsite comes with a picnic table and grill. Though Canyon de Chelly itself doesn't require an entrance fee, the campground charges $14 per night.

The good news: the cottonwood trees provide lots of welcome shade.

The bad news: well, just read the online reviews, which run from average to bad. Let me summarize. The campground is old and loud, the campsites are too close together, the restroom facilities (three of them, with sinks and toilets) sometimes work, sometimes don't. And there are too many wild dogs running through the campground looking for snacks. Fair enough, I would agree with most of that. Still, I've camped in a good many average to bad campgrounds over the years, and I've always found that I could survive one night, maybe two, depending on how much I wanted to hike the next day. So give Cottonwood a try. If you can't tolerate the bother, then pack up and head for the Holliday Inn.

AFTER THE FALL

Contrary to popular belief, Chaco's rich history didn't end when the Ancestral Puebloans abandoned the canyon. The Navajo moved South into the Four Corners area sometime between 1400 and 1525 A.D. Some of the Navajo oral histories place their arrival much earlier, even overlapping with the Puebloan presence at Chaco. At any rate, the Navajo began herding sheep, goats, and horses in the greater Chaco area at least by the late 1500s near Chacra Mesa, Kin Klizhin and other sites around the canyon.

The Navajo occupation of the Chaco area was ongoing when the Spanish arrived in New Mexico in the late 16th century. Possibly, the first recorded Spanish contact with the Navajo took place in 1583 when an expedition led by Antonio de Espejo encountered what he described as "Indios Serranos" (Mountain Indians) near Mount Taylor on his way to Zuni Pueblo. Many of the official records of the Spanish entrance into New Mexico were destroyed during the Pueblo Revolt of 1680 when the Puebloans laid siege to Santa Fe and captured the *Casas Reales* (government buildings). A good many Navajo had joined the Puebloans during the uprising and then later given them shelter after the Spanish returned in 1692, which increased tensions between the Spanish and Navajo, who by this time had a considerable presence in Chaco Canyon.

During the 17th and 18th centuries, as the Spanish spread out into the Four Corners area, they competed with the Navajo for land and resources. The situation became even more complicated after 1846, when Gen. Stephen Watts Kearney arrived in Santa Fe and claimed the city and the territory for the United States. Soon both Spanish and Anglo ranchers were competing with the Navajo in and around Chaco. One Anglo ranch, the LC operation, was headquartered just North of Penasco Blanco; another, the Carlisle Cattle Co. was located on Gallegos Wash to the North.

Whereas the Navajo were a bit wary of the Chaco ruins, at times associating them with places like the "White House" in some of their migration stories where evil things were said to have occurred, the Anglos had no such reservations. The first explicit report of Chaco Canyon by an American was in 1849 by First Lt. James H. Simpson of the U.S. Army Topographical Engineers. Simpson measured and described seven major and several smaller ruins, giving them names provided by his guides, who were both Native American and Spanish. His reports created a national interest in Chaco Canyon and its spectacular ruins, but it wasn't until after the Civil War that adventurers began visiting the canyon, intrigued by articles appearing in the popular press.

Enter Richard Wetherill, a Colorado rancher, explorer, and amateur archaeologist (or looter, some would say). Wetherill was famous for finding the abandoned Cliff Palace at Mesa Verde in 1888 and organizing an excavation, during which they dug, catalogued, and gathered artifacts that were later sold to the Historical Society of Colorado.

By the time he arrived in Chaco a few years later, Wetherill was already something of a national celebrity. Wetherill secured funding from wealthy New Yorkers Talbot and Frederick Hyde, and in 1896 began excavations at Pueblo Bonito. The Hyde Exploring Expedition, under the direction of F.W. Putnam of the American Museum of Natural History and Harvard University, removed massive amounts of artifacts from Bonito that were sent east to the Hydes and the American Museum of Natural History. Today I think it's fair to say that most people believe these artifacts should have remained in Chaco or at least in New Mexico museums. I certainly do.

Curiously, Wetherill remained in Chaco, building a homestead and a trading post, which he named the Bonito Trading Post. In its first manifestation the trading post was a rather humble one-room stone structure built out from the rear wall of Pueblo Bonito. An 1897 photograph, ostensibly taken by Wetherill, shows the structure under construction. Wetherill later expanded the trading post, building a homestead and a much larger trading post southwest of Pueblo Bonito, which he ran from the late 1890s until his death in 1910. To be precise, Wetherill was shot and killed by a Navajo man for reasons that are somewhat murky. He and his wife Marietta are buried in the small, fenced cemetery northwest of Pueblo Bonito.

But Wetherill wasn't the only American who tried to commercialize Chaco. There were at least two other active trading posts in the canyon, Chaco Canyon Trading Post at Pueblo del Arroyo, and Kimbeto Trading

Post above Escavada Wash just north of the canyon. The rush was on as ranchers, explorers and looters headed for the canyon. To prevent further looting or damage to prehistoric ruins, the United States Congress passed the Antiquities Act in 1906. The following year President Theodore Roosevelt created the "Chaco Canyon National Monument" on March 11, 1907, one of the first 18 national monuments created by Roosevelt.

In 1921 a National Geographic Society Expedition under the direction of Neil M. Judd, Curator of Archaeology at the United States National Museum, began excavating at Pueblo Bonito. By this time the science of dendrochronology for dating trees and other technological advances allowed for a more professional dig. During the excavation, the National Geographic Society funded preservation efforts to stabilize the ruin. It was the Judd team that discovered and catalogued the burials in Room 33, along with the thousands of turquoise beads, jewelry, seashells, and other ceremonial paraphernalia.

Also in 1921 another archaeologist, Edgar L. Hewett, began an excavation of Chetro Ketl. Over time Hewett created the Chaco Field School, a laboratory for archaeology students working at Chaco. Hewett's program was jointly run and funded by the School of American Research (now the School for Advanced Research) in Santa Fe and the University of New Mexico in Albuquerque. His students excavated over a hundred rooms at Chetro Ketl, finding similar, but fewer, precious stones and ceremonial paraphernalia than was found in Pueblo Bonito. In the 1930s Hewett and his students excavated Casa Rinconada and many other small one- and two-story dwellings in the canyon.

By the outbreak of World War II, Hewett's research station included a headquarters, a shop, a bathhouse, a photographic laboratory, storerooms, a dining room and kitchen, and eleven dormitories shaped like Navajo hogans. Back then Chaco had no visitor center. Instead, a caretaker was housed in a makeshift office near Pueblo Bonito. The first visitor center was built in 1957 as part of the "Mission 66" initiative to expand and upgrade national parks in the ten-year period leading up to the 50th anniversary of our national parks in 1966. The Chaco improvements included construction of a visitor center, housing for the staff, and a campground. In 2011 the visitor center was remodeled, with expanded museum exhibits, to its present form.

Over the last few decades there have been several major archaeology surveys and projects at Chaco, including the Chaco Project Archaeological

Survey 1971–1975 by the Chaco Center, a joint venture of the U.S. Department of Interior, the National Park Service, and the University of New Mexico, and the follow-up Additional Lands Archaeological Survey 1983–1984. Both surveys have been digitalized by the Chaco Research Archive and are available online at chacoarchive.org. I should also mention the National Park Service's Chaco Project 1971–1986 and the Chaco Stratigraphy Project, which began in 2004, directed by Patricia Crown and Chip Wills.

The Chaco Solstice Project, directed by Anna Sofaer, began in 1978. Sofaer and her contributors analyzed astronomical alignments at Chaco Canyon. Among other things, they found that basically all Chacoan Great Houses were oriented to the cycles of the sun or moon. They also found that, geographically, the Great Houses were located along lines related to these solar and lunar cycles. Their work supports the theory that ceremonies commemorating these solar and lunar cycles unified Chacoan society and solidified the rule of an elite who had knowledge of these recurring rhythms in the sky over Chaco Canyon and used that knowledge to maintain power. The Solstice Project team also mapped the maze of Chacoan roads surrounding Pueblo Alto on the North Mesa by using Lidar (Light Detection and Ranging technology).

The same technology was used by Kenneth B. Tankersley of the University of Cincinnati Anthropology and Geology departments to map a bank of dunes near the convergence of the Chaco and Escavada washes. In a research article on Ancestral Puebloan water management in the *Journal of Archeologic Sciences*, Tankersley identifies images of dunes, canals, and reservoirs used by Chacoans as water management systems. No doubt Chaco will continue to yield more secrets as Lidar and other new technologies become more widely used in the canyon.

On December 19, 1980, Chaco Canyon National Monument experienced a name change, becoming the Chaco Culture National Historical Park. At the same time 13,000 additional acres were added to the park. In 1987 Chaco became a UNESCO World Heritage Site.

Chaco still retains much of its grandeur seven centuries after its fall. Looking back from the long view of history it's clear that Chaco was a way station, not only for individuals and clans, but for an entire culture passing through, searching for the Center Place after emergence. The migration symbols everywhere on the walls of the canyon tell the story. We are all passing through—this place, this time, this life. All of us, all of our families, have our own history of migration. Indeed, the story of humans on this planet is a story of migration. This is what Chaco means to me. This is why I love the canyon.

Chaco Migration Symbol.

RECOMMENDED READING:

Carter, William B. *Indian Alliances and the Spanish in the Southwest, 750–1750*. Norman, Oklahoma: University of Oklahoma Press, 2009.

Crown, Patricia, ed. *The Pueblo Bonito Mounds of Chaco Canyon: Material Culture and Fauna*. Albuquerque, New Mexico: University of New Mexico Press, 2016.

Curry, Andrew. "DNA Offers Clues to Mysterious Crypt in Ancient Pueblo." Washington, DC: *National Geographic*, Feb. 21, 2017.

Goin, Peter, and Lucy R. Lippard. *Time and Time Again: History, Rephotography, and Preservation in the Chaco World*. Santa Fe, New Mexico: Museum of New Mexico Press, 2013.

Lekson, Stephen H. *The Chaco Meridian: One Thousand Years of Political and Religious Power in the Ancient Southwest*, Second Ed. New York: Rowman and Littlefield, 2015.

Lekson, Stephen H. *A History of the Ancient Southwest*. Santa Fe, New Mexico: School for Advanced Research Press, 2008.

Malville, J. McKim. *Guide to Prehistoric Astronomy in the Southwest*. Boulder, Colorado: Johnson Books, 2008.

Morrow, Baker H. and V.B. Price, eds. *Anasazi Architecture and American Design*. Albuquerque, New Mexico: University of New Mexico Press, 1997.

Plog, Stephen and Carrie Heitman. "Hierarchy and Social Inequality in the

American Southwest, A.D. 800–1200." Washington, DC: Proceedings of the National Academy of Sciences, *PNAS*, Nov.16, 2010,107(46) 19619-19626.

Roney, John R. "Prehistoric Roads and Regional Integration in the Chacoan System." In *Anasazi Regional Organization and the Chaco System*, edited by David E. Doyel, pp. 123-131. Papers of the Maxwell Museum of Anthropology 5. Albuquerque, NM: University of New Mexico Press, 1992.

Sofaer, Anna, ed. *Chaco Astronomy: An Ancient American Cosmology*. Santa Fe, New Mexico: Ocean Tree Books, 2007.

Tankersley, K.D. 2017. "Geochemical, Economic, and Ethnographic Approaches to the Evaluation of Soil, Salinity, and Water Management in Chaco Canyon, New Mexico." *Journal of Archaeologic Sciences: Reports* (April 2017) 12:378-383.

www.ingramcontent.com/pod-product-compliance
Lightning Source LLC
Chambersburg PA
CBHW070346100426
42812CB00005B/1447